COD

Edible

Series Editor: Andrew F. Smith

EDIBLE is a revolutionary series of books dedicated to food and drink that explores the rich history of cuisine. Each book reveals the global history and culture of one type of food or beverage.

Already published

Apple Erika Janik, *Avocado* Jeff Miller, *Banana* Lorna Piatti-Farnell, *Barbecue* Jonathan Deutsch and Megan J. Elias, *Beans* Nathalie Rachel Morris, *Beef* Lorna Piatti-Farnell, *Beer* Gavin D. Smith, *Berries* Heather Arndt Anderson, *Biscuits and Cookies* Anastasia Edwards, *Brandy* Becky Sue Epstein, *Bread* William Rubel, *Cabbage* Meg Muckenhoupt, *Cake* Nicola Humble, *Caviar* Nichola Fletcher, *Champagne* Becky Sue Epstein, *Cheese* Andrew Dalby, *Chillies* Heather Arndt Anderson, *Chocolate* Sarah Moss and Alexander Badenoch, *Cocktails* Joseph M. Carlin, *Coconut* Constance L. Kirker and Mary Newman, *Cod* Elisabeth Townsend, *Coffee* Jonathan Morris, *Corn* Michael Owen Jones, *Curry* Colleen Taylor Sen, *Dates* Nawal Nasrallah, *Doughnut* Heather Delancey Hunwick, *Dumplings* Barbara Gallani, *Edible Flowers* Constance L. Kirker and Mary Newman, *Edible Insects* Gina Louise Hunter, *Eggs* Diane Toops, *Fats* Michelle Phillipov, *Figs* David C. Sutton, *Foie Gras* Norman Kolpas, *Game* Paula Young Lee, *Gin* Lesley Jacobs Solmonson, *Hamburger* Andrew F. Smith, *Herbs* Gary Allen, *Herring* Kathy Hunt, *Honey* Lucy M. Long, *Hot Dog* Bruce Kraig, *Hummus* Harriet Nussbaum, *Ice Cream* Laura B. Weiss, *Jam, Jelly and Marmalade* Sarah B. Hood, *Lamb* Brian Yarvin, *Lemon* Toby Sonneman, *Lobster* Elisabeth Townsend, *Melon* Sylvia Lovegren, *Milk* Hannah Velten, *Moonshine* Kevin R. Kosar, *Mushroom* Cynthia D. Bertelsen, *Mustard* Demet Güzey, *Nuts* Ken Albala, *Offal* Nina Edwards, *Olive* Fabrizia Lanza, *Onions and Garlic* Martha Jay, *Oranges* Clarissa Hyman, *Oyster* Carolyn Tillie, *Pancake* Ken Albala, *Pasta and Noodles* Kantha Shelke, *Pickles* Jan Davison, *Pie* Janet Clarkson, *Pineapple* Kaori O'Connor, *Pizza* Carol Helstosky, *Pomegranate* Damien Stone, *Pork* Katharine M. Rogers, *Potato* Andrew F. Smith, *Pudding* Jeri Quinzio, *Rice* Renee Marton, *Rum* Richard Foss, *Saffron* Ramın Ganeshram, *Salad* Judith Weinraub, *Salmon* Nicolaas Mink, *Sandwich* Bee Wilson, *Sauces* Maryann Tebben, *Sausage* Gary Allen, *Seaweed* Kaori O'Connor, *Shrimp* Yvette Florio Lane, *Soda and Fizzy Drinks* Judith Levin, *Soup* Janet Clarkson, *Spices* Fred Czarra, *Sugar* Andrew F. Smith, *Sweets and Candy* Laura Mason, *Tea* Helen Saberi, *Tequila* Ian Williams, *Tomato* Clarissa Hyman, *Truffle* Zachary Nowak, *Vanilla* Rosa Abreu-Runkel, *Vodka* Patricia Herlihy, *Water* Ian Miller, *Whiskey* Kevin R. Kosar, *Wine* Marc Millon, *Yoghurt* June Hersh

Cod

A Global History

Elisabeth Townsend

REAKTION BOOKS

To Jeff, with much love and gratitude, always
To Dr George A. Rose, with enormous gratitude and appreciation
To Elizabeth Gawthrop Riely, also with thanks

Published by Reaktion Books Ltd
Unit 32, Waterside
44–48 Wharf Road
London N1 7UX, UK
www.reaktionbooks.co.uk

First published 2022
Copyright © Elisabeth Townsend 2022

Printed and bound in India by Replika Press Pvt. Ltd

A catalogue record for this book is available from the British Library

ISBN 978 1 78914 598 4

Contents

I

What Is a Cod?

North Atlantic cod has been the most commercially successful fish in the world. The abundant cod has been called a universal food that has fuelled the global exploration, and acutely affected the economies, of North America and Europe. It has provided work and sustenance for fishing families, been a staple dietary item in poorer countries and has also been consumed as an alternative to meat, especially for Christians on fast days. This worthy source of protein has stoked sailors on Viking expeditions, Portuguese explorers, fishing boats and pirate ships. And finally, it was one of the first valuable trading commodities.

The Atlantic cod, also known as *Gadus morhua*, is 4 to 5 million years old and has been integral to many of the most remarkable movements in world history. The preservation methods of the Vikings and the Basques had an enormous impact on their lives. Without dried cod, in the eighth century the Vikings would never have left the safety of their coastline. The cold, dry air of northern Norway is perfect for drying cod, enabling the Vikings' long voyages as far as North America. As early as the fifteenth century, salt-preserved cod may have done the same for the Basques. In their pursuit of whales far into the North Atlantic, they discovered cod. They used salt to preserve the cod rather than on the whales they had hoped to catch. The highly competitive search for a new spice route via the sea led to the discovery of seemingly boundless cod-fish and even produced the cod wars in the twentieth century. Cod's status as an indispensable food source for transatlantic voyages even influenced the slave trade. Today Nigerians have a love affair with dried cod, thanks to Norwegian generosity.

And now we are confronted with an existential threat to this essential food source. How can we continue sustainably to enjoy eating the magnificent cod without endangering it further, as we have, through hunting and resource exploitation, with whales and many others?

The Omnivorous Cod

No fish is as omnivorous as the great Atlantic cod. Unimaginable, inedible objects have been found in the stomachs of the Atlantic cod: a woman's wedding ring, a partial set of false teeth, scraps of wood and clothing, old boots, a cigarette case, oil cans and a rubber doll, among others. Many of these items may have fallen out of passenger ships, fishing boats and freighters. Cod are known for gulping whole shellfish, letting their stomach juices break down the interior meat. In one instance, indigestible sea clam shells were found in a cod's stomach in an orderly stack of six or seven.

Humans hunted for rare shells in cod stomachs, which is also where a giant deep-sea scallop shell was first found. Though it appears that cod have an undiscriminating palate, they much prefer the most beneficial foods for their species such as capelin and herring. When these are not available, they will also consume crabs, lobsters, big moon snails, brittle stars and various varieties of shrimp. They are cannibals,

The Atlantic cod, *Gadus morhua*, is 4 to 5 million years old.

Stockfish in a market in Abuja, Nigeria.

Lofoten fisherman with giant cod, 1910, photograph by Anders Beer Wilse, a Norwegian photographer who documented Norwegian life.

Giant cod, though rare, still exist, though they are not as common as when this photograph was taken of deckhand Agúst Ólafsson on an Icelandic trawler aboard the *Ver*, c. 1925.

even devouring their own offspring up to 17–20 centimetres (7–8 in.) long, along with other petite fish. Beyond believable is what Alan Davidson reports in *North Atlantic Seafood* – that in 1626 fishers caught a cod that had swallowed a 'book in three treatises', which was later given to the vice chancellor of the University of Cambridge.

The wedding ring is another story. In 1871 a Newfoundland fisherman was gutting a big codfish and about to salt it when the cod's recent dinner dropped on to the deck. Mixed in with the fish bones, shells and undigested food was a small, shiny object. This gold wedding ring was especially lustrous from the acidic gastric juices, but the inscription on the band's inside was illegible. A community newspaper investigation discovered the deceased owner – a traveller on the *Anglo Saxon*, a steamship that had gone astray and was destroyed near Chance Cove, Newfoundland. Most likely the woman's bones were spread by ocean currents, allowing a cod to guzzle the ring from the ocean floor.

It's not hard to imagine why cod would scoop up just about anything – especially the larger cod, which *were* enormous and voracious. They would snap up any unbaited or baited hook, especially if it was shiny. Perhaps the earliest evidence of a big cod was in 1838 on Georges Bank, when an 82-kilogram (180 lb) fish was landed. But in May 1895, a commercial fisherman hauled in the biggest cod on record – 96 kilograms (212 lb) and more than 1.8 metres (6 ft) long. Its nickname was the 'Patriarch Cod', and it was caught on a line off the Massachusetts coast.

Life and Sex

Cod are primarily found on the continental shelves of cold marine waters, usually at depths of less than 500–600 metres (1,640–1,970 ft). In the western Atlantic Ocean, the Atlantic cod range from Cape Hatteras, North Carolina, to both coasts of Greenland, including the Greenland Sea and the Labrador Sea. In the east, they stretch from the Bay of Biscay to the Arctic Ocean, including the Baltic Sea, the Barents Sea and the North Sea.

There are 26 Atlantic cod stocks identified by their geographic locations. Fish species like *Gadus morhua* are described as 'stocks', which are different groups or subpopulations, clustered in smaller bodies of coastal cod and then bigger bands of migratory cod. The heartiest stocks now include the Northeast Arctic (Barents Sea) and Icelandic cod. The most threatened is the mid-sized Southern Gulf of the St Lawrence group off New Brunswick and Quebec, Canada, which may become biologically extinct because of the increasing number of grey seals, which are 'real cod killers', explains marine biologist Professor George A. Rose. Those in Newfoundland-Labrador, West Greenland, New England and southern parts of the North Sea also are suffering, partly due to climate change. A less noticeable loss is of some of the smaller coastal clusters that may have just disappeared.

'Cod are a mobile species,' says Rose, a lifelong cod researcher born in Newfoundland. Cod are dominant partly because they are highly adaptable and live in different habitats. These cold-water ground fish fall into two groups – some are highly migratory, especially the larger stocks, while others have a smaller range limited to coastal bays and are more sedentary. 'There is literally a cod for every continental shelf habitat,' writes Rose. They adjust to local conditions including a broad array of feeding options, salinities and sea temperatures.

With intricate courtship and spawning behaviours, cod use their quite precise homing power to swim between their feeding and spawning areas. This fish is definitely a social species that travels in groups or shoals. Stocks may cover long distances to their breeding grounds – up to 320 kilometres

Atlantic cod range widely from northern Europe to North America.

(200 mi.) – or more locally. Some scientists believe larger fish behave as scouts, steering the migration.

While some cod stocks intermingle, others remain separate. Genetic differences have been found between coastal groups and among the major cod stocks in the northeast Atlantic. Coastal Newfoundland juveniles have blood with antifreeze glycoproteins for living in extremely cold waters, outgrowing the need for them when they reach about five years old and are able to move safely away from freezing waters. Coastal groups of cod reside in shallower water while others stay closer to the bottom in deeper water. That is unless they're spawning or chasing their prey, and then they may swim up to 100 metres (328 ft) from the bottom, closer to the surface, consuming almost anything but preferably capelin, a small, abundantly available fish. They hunt on stony grounds, including sand and gravel. They also scavenge in Irish moss and other seaweeds on deeper ledges near the shore.

When fishers haul in a cod, beyond its size, what do they see? First of all, it looks like an ordinary fish, but with one tiny distinctive difference – its chin barbel hangs from the

Both the trailing barbel on the Atlantic cod's (*Gadus morhua*) chin and the curved, pale lateral line from the gills to the tail differentiate it from other fish like haddock.

'Three Large Cod', 1910, photograph by Anders Beer Wilse.

lower jaw at the end of the chin. Almost a whisker, the trailing barbel has taste buds, as do the pelvic fin rays on the bottom of the fish and below the gills that help them identify food on the sea bed. Primarily a visual feeder, it needs light to find sustenance. Yet this big-bodied fish can smell odours from various live algae, fish and invertebrates with its barbel. Its big head uses its blunt-tipped, cone-shaped snout to poke and dig around the bottom, shove stones out of the way and even shovel away gravel by mouth. Strangely, it can't find food underneath sand. Cod have lots of small teeth along each jaw with which to devour prey.

Fishers would recognize the casual, curved, pale lateral line from the gills to the tail, which differentiates the cod from the haddock. There are three fins on top (dorsal), two fins on the bottom (anal) and two near the chest (pelvic). The unremarkable, almost square, whisk broom-shaped tail, protruding upper jaw and speckled markings set the cod apart from pollock. The body and head are swathed in tiny scales.

Codfish in a 16th-century Dutch fish market. Follower of Joachim Beuckelaer, *Fish Market*, *c.* 1595, oil on panel.

Similar to chameleons, individual cod can alter their exterior appearance, including their pattern, shading and hue, which is most likely life-saving camouflage. Their typical colour variations depend on the environment, location and diet, and are useful for concealment. Generally, the two predominant groups are grey-green-yellow and red-brown. Both groups include a whitish belly infused with a trace of the main body colour. Most cod have little speckles that drape the upper part of the body, fins, tail and sides of the head, but exclude the belly or snout.

On the inside, the firm, flaky, mild flesh is a result of what the cod eat, contributing to their taste and texture. They are nutritious and easy to cook in many different ways, and because their flesh is less oily than salmon, for example, they are also good for drying and salting. For centuries, snout-to-tail consumption has been common with this fish. Some fishers favour the head with its tasty cheeks and throat muscles, also called 'tongues'. The head and bones make fish broth for soups and stews, and the Dutch bake the tail end of a big cod. Cod roe, a delicacy, is an ingredient in Norwegian waffles, and served on toast or bread after being boiled and fried by Flemish fishermen. Even the air bladders, or 'cod sounds', used for buoyancy, are edible. But today most consumers enjoy the meaty bodies available at the fish counter.

The delicate flavour comes from a variety of sources. Cod have insatiable appetites, constantly searching for something edible. Of course, what they eat depends on what prey are in their part of the ocean and their stage of growth. Cod larvae concentrate on phytoplankton for nourishing food, while adolescent cod consume small crustaceans. Medium-sized cod devour small fish and bigger crustaceans. Large cod eat fish, especially schooling fishes including alewife, capelin, herring and menhaden. They like crab and squid too, which fishermen catch as bait, as well as whelks and other larger crustaceans.

Clicking, grunting, thumping, knocking and drum-like growls – these can't be sounds from a cod? Yet, scientists have discovered that cod, along with over eighty other fish, make sounds. Their research shows that cod can hear sound and detect the direction from which it is coming. They identify sound via the swim bladder–inner ear complex. The air or swim bladder is also involved in making sounds. Muscles around the swim bladder cause vibrations, including clicking and a variety of other sounds. Cod also use sounds to threaten predators when disturbed or frightened. This ability helps during the breeding season since males appear to make noise to attract females, though both sexes produce sounds. Scientists hypothesize that stronger males with larger muscles compete with each other to drum more loudly in order to entice females and to threaten other males. Research indicates human-made sounds in oil or gas exploration and drilling might disrupt the sounds fish make for mating, as well as endanger the fish. Trawling as well as immobile fishing nets like gillnets break up spawning gatherings, inducing a chronic stress reaction. The delay can harm egg fertilization and survival.

'It has been calculated that if no accident prevented the hatching of the eggs and if each egg reached maturity, it would take only three years to fill the sea so that you could walk across the Atlantic dry-shod on the backs of cod,' wrote the nineteenth-century French author Alexandre Dumas in the *Le Grande Dictionnaire de cuisine* in 1873. Of course, this was a fantasy. But it is true that cod produce a whopping number

Zach Whitener, research associate at the Gulf of Maine Research Institute, holding a cod while collecting samples for a study about the effect of changing temperatures on fish.

of eggs. The largest recorded number of eggs produced by a 140-centimetre (55 in.) female was 12 million. Five million eggs can be produced by a 50-centimetre (20 in.) female cod in just one mating season. Females, depending on their size, can release between 1 and 4 million eggs annually, but they only release 5 to 25 per cent of their entire egg supply each time. A female can produce several batches of eggs each season, but with different partners. During a few weeks in captivity, she can produce about twenty batches, each comprising thousands of eggs. Cod stocks spawn once a year, primarily in late winter, spring and summer months – some earlier, some later. The timing takes advantage of zooplankton growth on which young cod feed. But it takes a bit of work for this all to happen.

During the spawning season, cod migrate to warmer waters, especially during the winter and spring, staying there between three weeks to three months. Both males and females have to be sexually mature, the age of which varies for different cod populations, depending on growth rates and sea temperatures. For instance, some females are not ready to spawn until they are six to eleven years old. Others are mature at two years old. Aggressive behaviour by males begins three weeks before spawning. There's a courtship, of course, which involves males drumming to attract females, and scientists hypothesize that a female selects her mate based on which is the strongest and loudest. Males also raise their dorsal fins and embellish their bodies' lateral bends. And at night, when spawning usually happens, the female rises in the water column and the male swims over her and then below her so they are belly to belly – the missionary position if we're anthropomorphizing. At this point, there are many pairs of spawning cod in the same area, all swimming in circles. Then the male grasps the female's sides with his pelvic fins to situate himself below her in the 'ventral mount position'. How does the actual fertilization happen? According to the Danish biologist G. M. Dannevig, who in 1887 seems to have been the first to report this information while observing spawning cod in hatcheries, with their genital openings facing each other, the male releases his sperm, which floats up to the batch of the female's eggs. It takes about ten seconds. And *voilà*! Energetic swimming around in the water ensures the eggs are fertilized, though not always by the intended male.

Forget parenting. Cod do not nurture their offspring. They are broadcast spawners, releasing their fertilized buoyant eggs to drift on their own in the ocean currents. It is fortunate that the females are so fertile, since it is possible that only one egg out of 1 to 4 million will survive to adulthood. It would help if the adult cod did not eat them, but cod eggs are not distinct from those of haddock, nor are the larvae. They are also eaten by other fish and sea birds. The eggs are sensitive to temperature, and may float into water that's too warm or cold. Rose describes the eggs as 'very beautiful, tiny little jewels in the ocean'.

After incubating for one to eight weeks, the upper sea-floating eggs hatch and become larvae. They primarily guzzle phytoplankton, and once they become juveniles, swim to the seabed and begin gobbling invertebrates.

Sometimes called the 'world's largest maternity ward', the windy Vestfjord is the most significant spawning ground in northern Europe. It is between the Norwegian mainland and an archipelago, the Vesterålen and Lofoten islands, where the latter's fishery has thrived since the Stone Age. For more than a thousand years, Norsemen have hauled cod in this fjord, selling stockfish and cod liver oil. In the northwestern Atlantic, spawning takes place primarily in southern New England, the Gulf of Maine and further north. In large clusters and feeding along the way, during spawning season, the cod's journey could be 320 kilometres (200 mi.) or more.

Spawning is a major reason that cod migrate. While some travel great distances, there are other groups that do not wander more than several dozen miles. A European cod holds the record for what humans can confirm is the longest journey – from the North Sea, by a fish that was tagged in June 1957, to the Grand Banks, where it was captured in January 1962 – a transatlantic trek of about 3,200 kilometres (1,990 mi.). However, we don't know why it made this journey. We do know that there are regular seasonal migrations throughout the year prompted by weather changes.

How long can cod live? From a few hours as eggs to over twenty years. Estimates range from 20 to 25 years, but most today are rarely older than fifteen years. Scientists have discovered that cod have an ear bone or otolith in their skull that can be used to decipher age, much like counting the rings on tree stumps. Cutting the otolith crossways reveals light and dark zones – a pair equals a year of life. Albert C. Jensen, author of *The Cod* (1972), describes otoliths as 'pearly-white calcium carbonate bodies that look something like narrow lima beans' and aid their balance.

The adult cod doesn't need to be a fast swimmer to avoid predators, because there are so few – primarily harp and harbour seals, and brawny sharks. That said, cod are susceptible to fourteen fish species – most often other cod, spiny dogfish, flounder and sea raven; sometimes skate, hake and short-finned squid, too. In eastern Canada, grey seals especially are fond of cod. Cod larvae and juveniles are vulnerable to smaller predators, such zooplankton, and other cod, dogfish, halibut and squid, respectively. Cod use clicking sounds and a sudden swimming movement to escape predators, but they do not have the horizontal line of dark fatty tissue that gives other

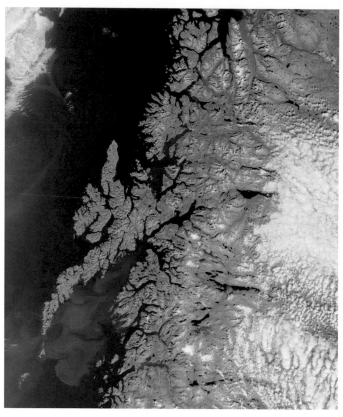

Norway's Lofoten archipelago, north of the Arctic Circle, seen here in the bottom far left, has historically been the home of one of the world's richest cod stocks.

fish high-speed access to energy. But when the tables are turned, writes Rose, 'They are a surprise predator, with a great burst of speed during attack – like a leopard.' Of course, human predators are another story.

Origins

In many coastal fishing communities, for centuries cod was simply called *fish*, or a translation of that generic term. The origin of the name 'cod' is unclear. It was scientifically named in 1758 by the Swedish botanist Carolus Linnaeus, taking the Greek word for fish, *gados*, and the Latin for cod, *morua*. This once spectacularly plentiful marine fish is in the family Gadidae of the order Gadiformes. There are two or three other species in the genus *Gadus* with the Atlantic cod – both the Pacific walleye pollock (*Gadus chalcogrammus*) and the Pacific cod (*Gadus macrocephalus*). It's unclear whether the Greenland, or rock, cod (*Gadus ogac*) is the same species or just closely related to the Pacific cod.

The origins of the actual fish seem more distinct, thanks to fossils and science. Cod are native or endemic to the North

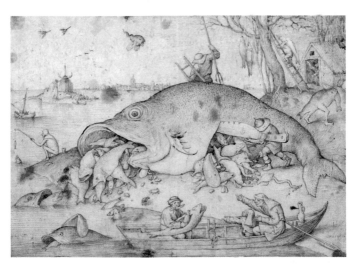

Pieter Bruegel the Elder, *The Big Fish Eat the Little Fish*, 1556, brush and pen and grey and black ink. This expressive engraving evokes the omnivorous cod.

Atlantic Ocean and belong to a larger scientific group called gadoids. Gadoids emerged in the eastern North Atlantic around 50 to 65 million years ago according to genetic analysis and fossils discovered in Greenland and the North Atlantic. The shifting of landmasses and seas allowed the interchange of marine fauna and species, including the Northern cod's favourite food, capelin. These movements allowed the cod's ancestors to cross to the Pacific Ocean from the North Atlantic Ocean about 3.5 million years ago, eventually becoming the Pacific cod. About 2 million years ago, Atlantic cod travelled again to the Pacific, evolving into the Pacific walleye pollock. Scientists think the Pacific cod returned to the Atlantic roughly 100,000 years ago, surviving as the Greenland or rock cod. Also, haddock and pollock probably developed as a gadoid ancestor.

The well-known haddock and Atlantic pollock, or saithe, are often mistakenly labelled cod. Other close-living relatives in the Gadidae family include saffron cod, pouts, poutings, poor cod, whiting and the siblings polar cod and Arctic cod. Clearly, 'cod' is not used exclusively for the Atlantic cod. Other species also may be informally identified as cod, such as Atlantic tomcod, black cod (sable) or blue cod. Even hake are close relatives of cod and in the order of Gadiformes. In the southern hemisphere, there are species designated as cod that are not closely related.

There are also regional variations for 'cod', as illustrated by the apocryphal story related by Alan Davidson in *North Atlantic Seafood* about how the New England word 'scrod' came into use. The esteemed historic hotel Boston Parker House opened in 1855. It prided itself on its daily super-fresh fish. But the manager never knew which variety of fish would be delivered on any given day. So he created the word 'scrod' as a generic name on the menu. Now 'scrod' is used for young cod, while young haddock is described as 'schrod'. They are merely separated by the unpronounced 'h'. (Don't be surprised if people still call haddock 'scrod'.) A young cod is also called a codling.

The many names for the North Atlantic cod are indicative of how widespread it is as a food source. There are also differences in the names of fresh-caught, dried or salted fish. The French use *morue* if it is salted and *cabillaud* if fresh. The Spanish term *bacalao* (and *bakailoa* in Basque) denotes salted cod, which became part of the Basque diet when intrepid Basques fished for whales in the cold and dangerous North Atlantic, possibly around 1000 CE. Their access to salt allowed them to bring it home preserved. Italians (*baccalà*) and Portuguese (*bacalhau*) used the same preservation method, making it a dietary staple. *Bacalhau* is so popular in Portugal that it has become the national dish. The Danish, Swedish and Norwegians use the name *torsk*. The Norwegians also use *skrei*, derived from an old Norse word that is now used for fresh Norwegian Arctic cod, which is sometimes both dried and

Fisherman landing Icelandic cod. It's still dangerous work.

salted, now called *klippfisk* or klipfish. Russians use the word *treska*, Icelanders employ another old Norse term for cod, *þorskur*, while the Faroese call it *toskur*. Stockfish, or *stokkfisk* (also known as *tørrfisk*) in Norwegian, is unsalted cod that is dried on racks out in the cold open air.

Stockfish and salted cod fed the Europeans as they searched for more plentiful fishing grounds. Salted cod enabled the Basques to sail hundreds of miles from the Iberian Peninsula in search of whales. Later, dried cod fuelled the Viking voyages as they plundered the new territories for profit, power and more land. Stockfish and improved shipbuilding techniques permitted the Vikings to sail all the way to North America.

2

Cod Fuelled the Age of Discovery, 500–1500

Homo sapiens were hungry. The desire for fish grew as the European population in the late tenth and early eleventh centuries outpaced available agricultural production. Hunger was one of the strongest motivators for humans to venture out into the unknown open seas to catch fish, as was an intense craving for wealth, power and status. Whether it was the Vikings hunting for wealth and new lands, fuelled by stockfish, or the Basque fishers seeking whales and finding cod instead, or the Germans in northern Europe dominating the dried cod trade, Europeans were on the move.

For over a thousand years, Norwegians have been harvesting cod. The first fishery to have an international market generating revenue was around the northern chain of Lofoten and Vesterålen Islands on the stormy Norwegian Sea. The Norwegians' income source was dried cod or stockfish. The climate around these islands was perfect for drying this non-oily species of fish, the earliest food preservation method used 100,000 years ago by Stone Age hunters.

During the Middle Ages and early modern period, the indigenous Sámi and Norwegian subsistence farmers struggled to feed themselves and their families, living off fishing in the winter, raising some sheep and cattle, and finding mountainside fields inland on which to grow hay in the summer. This combination of a 'farmer-fisherman' household is described as having 'one green foot and one blue foot' by Reidar Bertelsen, a Norwegian historical archaeologist, who stresses that 'the green foot (farmer) was female and the blue (fisherman) was male.'

To catch the coastal cod, Stone Age locals used hooks created from bone and horn with stone sinkers on a line of vegetable fibre, horsehair and sheep guts, and used nets in shallower water. These handlines – a single line with a hook – were also used in the deeper sea with boats. They worked well with cod, which are insatiable eaters and do not struggle once caught. Stockfish, air-dried cod, became a reliable, year-round source of food. Middens in one Lofoten community identify cod as the primary catch; leftover headless cod backbones meant that most of the cod had been stockfish. From the Middle Ages, cod was eaten by ordinary folk in stews or boiled, but the nobility were treated to various green sauces on their fresh or salt cod, based on ground parsley, bread, salt and vinegar.

Stockfish made exploration possible for Vikings, who were experts in ship design, construction, sailing and navigation. Some Vikings were ruthless and volatile; they raided and pillaged wherever they went. From the late eighth century to the late eleventh century, Vikings with deep-seated wanderlust travelled across large swathes of eastern, central, northern and western Europe, and eventually landed on the northeastern coast of North America. Also known as Norsemen or Norse, the Vikings had a 'powerful warrior culture in which personal prestige, kin ties, and wealth were of consuming importance', writes Brian Fagan, author of *Fish on Friday*. In the late eighth century, what the Vikings couldn't make themselves, they went elsewhere to steal and later to trade for.

Stockfish, eaten as a kind of hardtack, made both of these possible.

Norse invasions of Britain, starting in 793, led to settlement and colonization. The native Britons learned from the Norse, who, though less developed in some ways, were highly skilled seamen. Until the inhabitants of Britain learned from these Nordic invaders how to manoeuvre boats and fish at sea, anadromous species such as salmon, sturgeon and shad were the only saltwater species they ate. By 800 the Vikings had raided Scotland, Ireland and France.

If the Norsemen didn't have salt and needed it, they knew where to get it – in the salt marshes at Noirmoutier, an island off the coast west of Nantes, France. In 860 Ermentarius, an English-born monk serving there, wrote:

> The number of ships grows: the endless stream of Vikings never ceases to increase. Everywhere Christians are victims of massacres, burnings, plunderings: the Vikings conquer all in their path, and no one resists them: they seize Bordeaux, Périgueux, Limoges, Angoulême and Toulouse. Anger, Tours and Orléans are annihilated and an innumerable fleet sails up the Seine.

But the Vikings were explorers and went much further afield than Europe. An oft-told story is that of Erik the Red and his son Leif Erikson's expeditions beyond the Shetland and Faroe Islands to Iceland, Greenland and on to Labrador, Newfoundland and northeastern North America between 800 and 1000. These Norsemen were probably the first northern Europeans to discover America, preceding Christopher Columbus by five hundred years. Though there are remnants of Viking houses in L'Anse aux Meadows, Newfoundland, from 1000, they did not establish any permanent settlements. In

The beautiful archipelago of Lofoten is the home of Norway's cod-fishing industry.

both Newfoundland and Labrador, cod migrate to the coast in the summer rather than the winter – this made it impossible to be both a farmer and a fisherman as in Scandinavia.

How could the restless Vikings survive such long voyages? The protein-rich stockfish fed them during these voyages – a kilogram of stockfish contains about the same amount of protein as 5 kilograms (11 lb) of fresh cod. Generations of Norwegians knew how to fish and how to dry cod, and stockfish had been produced in Iceland and Norway for trading in northern Europe at least as early as the 800s. Both countries had the necessary cold, dry climate for stockfish. One could eat it like hardtack or jerky. But it could also be rehydrated and boiled.

There is written evidence of stockfish trading as a commodity in Icelandic sagas. It is mentioned in the 1200s in *Egil's Saga*, a story about the clan of an Icelandic farmer, poet and Viking who emigrated from Norway because of a feud with the king. It covers the clan's lives from about 850 to 1000. The

A faering, named for the Norwegian word for 'four-oaring', is an open boat with two pairs of oars, sometimes with a small sail, and found mostly in western and northern Scandinavia. Fishing in those waters was dangerous work. Fishers could easily get caught in a sudden storm swamping these small double-ended rowboats, and drown along rocky coasts.

Norwegian stockfish on a drying rack. Norway, Iceland and the Faroe Islands have the ideal cold, dry weather for drying cod.

tale shows the early use and value of this prized food source that was so easily preserved. Norwegian farmers were the primary settlers of Iceland, who replicated their stockfish production in the similar climate.

While both the Norwegians and Icelanders had the cold, dry wind to preserve cod, the Basques had salt. Basques were roaming the Atlantic long before anyone even knew they were there, perhaps as early as the fifteenth century. These intrepid, skilled fishermen are contenders for the first Europeans to reach North America after the Vikings. This native ethnic group from Basque Country – north-central Spain to southwest France – searched distant unknown waters for what the Europeans loved eating: the whale, which had been overfished in nearby seas.

The Oseberg ship, a speedy, agile Viking longboat built for war and exploration, is in Norway's Viking Ship Museum. The sails supplemented with oars made it more versatile.

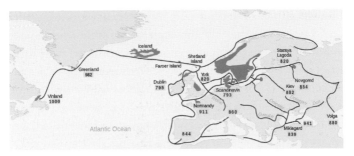

Territories and explorations of the Vikings.

Like most fishermen, the Basques kept their fishing grounds secret. Chasing the schools of herring and cod that whales ate, the Basques found enormous groups of cod that when salted became a food source that remained edible throughout extended voyages. It also became a new, longer-lasting product to sell, keeping even longer than dried fish, salted red-meat whale or herring. Keep it dry and out of hot, humid weather and it might last two years or more.

Just as the world was on the verge of a seismic shift in food supply, there was an unnoticed whisper of change in the relationship between codfish and humans. In Scotland in about 800, the local diet changed: suddenly cod bones show up in the historical record, as do remnants of seabirds that nest on distant islands. These traces suggest that the Scottish people discovered how to use boats sturdy enough to catch cod in deep open waters and explore new islands. It could also mean that the Vikings' arrival in Scotland led to innovative shipbuilding and deep-sea fishing. Another trace shows up in Belgium in the mid-900s, when cod and herring appear.

But these shudders turned into a seismic shift in Europe between 950 and 1050. There was a sudden spike in marine fish consumption, including some cod and a lot of herring. As the Norse invaded and settled in northern Europe, they brought with them the consumption of marine fish, especially cod. Once again they also brought their shipbuilding, navigation and fishing abilities to each new community. It took bigger ships and special know-how to fish in open water. Around the first millennium, bigger ships were constructed, allowing fishing beyond the shoreline. They were just in time for the Europeans, who had overfished their local freshwater stocks and were searching for new sources.

The larger ships were providential because, at about the same time, new towns surfaced in northern Europe, requiring increased food supplies beyond what they produced themselves. Instead of easily spoiled fresh fish, the new town dwellers added long-lasting dried cod and salted herring to their diet. It was a profound change to the diet of northern Europeans.

In England at around the same time, consumption of cod increased when eating ocean-caught fish became more popular than eating freshwater fish. Cod was a fish for which the English didn't even have a name, according to author Michael Pye. And thanks to the archaeologists who scrutinize fish bones, we know that shortly thereafter it was being eaten all over the country. In England and Belgium, much of the cod and other marine fish was caught in the nearby North Sea in the 800s to 1100s. The fish was probably not preserved but eaten fresh. By the 1200s, inhabitants of both England and Europe were consuming dried cod from Norway and the Baltic Sea. At the same time, the French were also eating more marine fish. In *The Edge of the World*, Pye declares, 'Fishing at sea was, for the first time, feeding the land.'

The increased demand for dried cod or stockfish was also generated by two organizations in the fourteenth century – the Hanseatic League and the Christian Church – raising it to the level of a commodity. Beginning in the late 1100s, a handful of

Drying Icelandic cod in Seyðisfjörður, 20th century.

northern German towns banded together as a merchant guild to combat piracy and develop maritime trade. The Hanseatic League, based in Lübeck, Germany, dominated seafaring commerce for several centuries throughout Europe's northern coast and as far north as Bergen, Norway, flourishing there for about four hundred years. In key coastal towns, they traded grains, fur, metals, salt, wood, cloth and other commodities for dried cod. The league's enclaves ranged from Novgorod to London, Iceland and Norway. From its segregated settlement on the dock of Bergen, it exercised a near monopoly on stockfish from northern Norway, and tried to control other bulk commodities such as salted fish.

The growth in stockfish trade coincided with another increase in desire for cod as well as other fish. In the 1300s, the Church required that almost half the year be dedicated to abstinence from meat (and sex). Catholic monastic diets became more extravagant while their appetites became more sophisticated, as did the desires of the aristocracy, whose wealth was gradually increasing. Cod took the dwindling

Salted cod, shown here in Iceland, fuelled many sailors through the centuries.

Norwegian cod fishing boat, 1924, photograph by Anders Beer Wilse.

herring's place at the table, as a vast, seemingly endless resource. It even became a major food for armies and expanding navies, as it was lightweight and easy to carry. Lent, with its six-week diet restrictions, was especially challenging, and people relied on a lot of different fish. Indeed, although stockfish and salted cod were associated with abstinence and penitence, they were certainly eaten regularly during this period, as was smoked cod. Coastal dwellers ate fresh cod.

Two medieval books reveal how cod was prepared in France. In the early 1300s, the author of *Le Viandier de Taille-vent* suggests, 'Salt cod is eaten with mustard sauce or with melted fresh butter over it.' While Guillaume Tirel, nicknamed Taillevent, is often mistakenly credited as the cookbook's author, he was in fact an influential chef in French royal households, and is after whom the famous Paris restaurant, among others, is named. (*Le Viandier* was already in existence before Tirel was born, but he used and edited the cookbook.) A 1393 medieval French guidebook for women about household management, *Le Ménagier de Paris*, written for the author's teen-aged bride, suggests, 'When salt fish is not adequately soaked, it tastes too salty; and yet soak it too much and it does not taste good; therefore, whoever buys it ought to test it by biting off and tasting a bit.' But fresh cod was cooked with wine and served with a 'jance' sauce of spices, such as ginger or pepper, onions, verjuice (sorrel and plum juices) and maybe wine and garlic.

The demand for fresh fish was increasing. People wanted more variety and better quality. Sometimes other species of salted fish were spoiled and infected with insects. Coastal monasteries hired full-time fishers to provide steady deliveries of pristine marine fish. Some of the best records of cod consumption come from these religious communities. Splurging extravagant amounts on fresh sea fish, in 1405 the priory in Peterborough, England, also paid handsomely for stockfish and salted herring. Before Easter, a Maundy Thursday banquet included twenty codling (young cod), two turbot, six greenfish, two great rays, 1,500 whelks, one fresh salmon and an eel.

In the 1400s, stockfish was much preferred over salted herring by all economic classes. Cod was a more dependable catch and, dried and salted, easy to preserve. Now the Italians joined their French neighbours and developed a taste for dried cod.

In 1431, while sailing from Crete to Flanders, a Venetian merchant sea captain, Pietro Querini, was blown off course in a ferocious storm. His ship was destroyed, but he and eleven seamen drifted in a lifeboat to the North Sea in winter. Starving and near death, they landed on the rocky southernmost Lofoten island where they were eventually found. By May 1432 they had recovered enough to return home to

Italy – this time by land – bringing a large number of stockfish with them. Captain Querini wrote a journal about his experience. In it he described how their rescuers prepared stockfish, pounded thin and drenched with butter, which nourished them back to health. Querini eventually became the first importer of stockfish, *stoccafisso*, to Italy. (In 2012, *Querini*, a lyric opera, and certainly the only one about stockfish, by the Norwegian composer Henning Sommerro, based on Querini's report, was performed in Lofoten, to acclaim by the *Financial Times*.)

As the demand for cod grew and the herring migrations wavered, English fishers began to look for more new cod sources. They set sail for Iceland. (They never seem to have encountered the Basques.) Iceland-bound ships from England were sure to cross paths with the Hanseatic League vessels, sparking early conflict over cod. Bristol, a centre for Iceland's stockfish trade that relied on a steady Christian demand for fish, was a prosperous port, and strategically located despite the journey down the perilous Bristol Channel. A handful of

Hans Dahl, *Fjord with Sailing Boat*, before 1937, oil on canvas. Dahl was a Norwegian painter of fjords and landscapes.

Bristol merchants purchased dried cod as early as the 1420s. There is some speculation that in the 1480s Bristol ships found North America before Christopher Columbus, but then, like the Basques, no one was revealing the source of the cod. An untold number of Bristol ships continued delivering lucrative stockfish from Iceland throughout the century. That is, until the Hanse stopped the Bristol traders from dealing with the Icelandic fisheries in the 1470s. A couple of decades later, when the fracas had faded, the Hanse suggested restarting Icelandic trading, but the Bristol merchants had moved on to flourishing western North Atlantic fisheries. Most importantly, Basque, English, French and Portuguese fishers had happened upon the Grand Banks of Newfoundland, the mother lode of cod fishing grounds in the bountiful western North Atlantic. Whether it was because of ancient tales shared among sea captains, unpredictable wind patterns or serendipity, we will never know.

While this completely unexpected new source of fish – and wealth in the form of the silver backs of cod rather than gold – stoked the European imagination, there emerged a new maritime source of riches, a water route to the spices and gold of Asia. Many merchants wanted to free themselves from the rulers of the profitable overland spice trade – Genoa and Venice. Better-designed ships, more intrepid sailors and financing by European monarchs certainly magnified the desire to explore the Asian world. At the same time, the European population was swiftly expanding on the western European peninsula and the Little Ice Age descended on Europe, shrinking growing seasons and intensifying erratic bad weather. For many reasons, the soon-to-be-famous explorers were on the move.

In 1497 John Cabot, a Genoese sea captain like Columbus, claimed Newfoundland for English monarch Henry VII, for which he gave Cabot an annual pension of £20 sterling. Cabot, a year older than Columbus, was also searching for a waterway to China for gold and gems that would enrich the British. His westward-bound ship sailed from Bristol, a city known as the departure point for expeditions throughout the North Atlantic.

On 18 December 1497, one of the few reports of Cabot's voyage was written by Milan's envoy in London, Raimondo di Soncino, to the Duke of Milan, about John Cabot's return on 6 August:

He began to sail toward the Oriental regions . . . and having wandered about considerably, at last he struck mainland [It is not clear whether it was Cape Breton, Labrador or Newfoundland, but the settlements are reported to have had the English flag.] . . . they affirm that that [sic] sea is covered with fishes, which are caught not only with the net but with baskets, a stone being tied to them in order that the baskets may sink in the water. And this I heard the said Master John relate.

On the same trip, the Englishmen realized the value of these New World fish and said their ships 'will bring so many fishes that this kingdom will no longer have need of Iceland, from which country there comes a very great store of fish which are called stock-fish'.

Early explorers like Cabot were sustained by air-dried cod and salt cod. Later, there is evidence of how salt cod was cooked on naval ships. In the mid-1500s, the crew of the *Mary Rose*, a British vessel in Portsmouth, preparing for battle with the French, got a welcome break with a fish-day meal of 'poor John', another name for salt-cured cod. For 24 hours, the salt cod soaked in large water-filled tanks. Then it was portioned into cloth bags which were loaded into wooden buckets and lugged below decks to the galley to be boiled in cauldrons. Each sailor received one-fourth of a 60-centimetre (24 in.) salt cod, along with bread, butter, cheese and beer. Salt cod also shows up much later, in 1623, in Shakespeare's *The Tempest*, when a smelly fisherman is described as 'not of the newest Poor-John'.

In spite of the marine wealth at their fingertips, the search for the water route to Asia continued. One Portuguese adventurer, Vasco da Gama, set out to find the eastern passage on his first voyage of 1497–9 and became the first European to sail to India. Supported by King Manuel I of Portugal, he steered his ship along Africa's west coast to the tip of the Cape of Good Hope, up the east coast to Mozambique, then crossed the Indian Ocean to Calicut, India. And he brought back the requisite boatload of precious spices. This discovery and ensuing dominance of the route to India resulted in a

'If there were more world, we would get there': world map of the Portuguese empire and statue of Henry the Navigator, in the miniature park Portugal dos Pequenitos, Coimbra. Portuguese discoveries, exploration, contacts and conquests between 1336 and 1543 extended to the Spice Islands and China.

A Spanish caravel with two lateen sail rigs and a headsail, seen here in a detail from a painting by Frederic Leonard King, 1934–5. Essential to the Age of Discovery, caravels were invented by the Portuguese and were more manoeuvrable.

global empire for Portugal. Wherever the Portuguese landed, salt cod, the staple of the voyagers' diet, became part of the cuisine, far from the fish's geographical range.

Cod did not go unnoticed by the Portuguese in North America, where they were laying claim to new territories in Newfoundland (just like Cabot's competing claim for the English). In the early 1500s, Newfoundland salt cod could be found in Portuguese ports, not to mention in Normandy's Rouen market. Mark Kurlansky, author of *Cod* (1997), writes, 'By midcentury, 60 percent of all fish eaten in Europe was cod.' This would continue through the next two centuries.

Given the abundance of marine resources, it is not surprising that a curved peninsula in the midst of cod-fishing grounds would eventually be associated with this famous fish. It was discovered accidentally while another Italian, Giovanni da Verrazzano, was exploring the North American coast around 1524–7. Hunting for a route to China for the

French crown, Verrazzano called it Pallavisino, in honour of an Italian general. Indeed, the outline of Cape Cod, Massachusetts, is on one of Verrazzano's maps, but without the current name.

The European land grab of North America continued 42 years after Columbus, when the Breton explorer Jacques Cartier seized what is now Canada for France in 1534. He too was driven to find the path to Asia. In an oft-repeated story, Cabot encountered a thousand Basque whalers in the mouth of the St Lawrence River – but there is no concrete evidence of Basques in these numbers in the North Atlantic. The first solid proof was the discovery of the ruins of a Basque whaling station on the Labrador coast from the 1530s. It is very possible that much earlier than these well-publicized voyagers, the Basque, English, French and Portuguese fishers had tracked down the richest cod grounds in the New World – the Grand Banks of Newfoundland. After Cabot's voyages to North America, the competition was on.

3

Cod Wars and the Expansion of Fishing, 1500–1976

As the quest to discover channels to East Asia continued, so too did the quest for cod. In North America, the rediscovery of the Grand Banks off Newfoundland and Labrador in the late 1400s proved them to be the most plentiful source of cod until their collapse in the early 1990s. The Vikings stumbled on them first and their rediscovery soon turned the cod fishery upside down, inviting a swarm of Europeans.

No wonder. The nourishing continental shelves of the Grand Banks with their enticing stew of rich nutrients produced a seemingly inexhaustible stock of *Gadus morhua*. Located off southern Newfoundland, where the warm Gulf Stream intersects the cold Arctic waters of the Labrador Current, these underwater banks resemble the mesas in the American Southwest. The ledges are not completely submerged and have underwater plateaus with water as shallow as 50 metres (164 ft). These rocks are part of North American landmasses and are roughly 200 nautical miles from Newfoundland's shore. The shelves are described as 'underwater shoulders of continental landmasses' by George A. Rose. The fifteenth-century Grand Banks had an enormous repository of fish, the most abundant of any of the cod fisheries.

At the end of the 1400s, some Europeans in this age of exploration were turning to the New World in search of new fish sources because their stocks had been practically destroyed. Merchants craved more lucrative fish sources and the Basques' preferred catch, the whale, had been fished out and they needed another seafood for hungry customers on the Continent. The French, Basque, Portuguese and English fishermen all sailed to the Labrador and Newfoundland shorelines. Throughout the 1500s, the French commanded the fisheries as a result of Jacques Cartier claiming Canada for France in 1534. There were also some Portuguese vessels. But it was Britain that challenged the French, in one of many feuds over several centuries. By the late 1500s, the English fleet had dislodged the French from much of the convenient Newfoundland inshore or close-to-the-shore fishing, taking

Plentiful beyond anyone's wildest dreams, codfish were once thought to be inexhaustible.

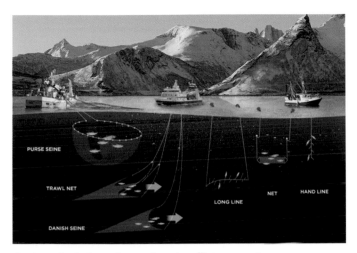

Catch methods for cod range from handlining to various nets.

the choice drying sites. But all the French had to do was shift to the north and west coasts to continue their land-based fishery. They also dominated the Grand Banks, where there was plenty of cod for their 'green' fishery which specialized in salted and undried cod.

The North American fishing season was kicked off with a fierce spring race from Europe to Newfoundland – the first vessel to arrive there got the best fishing and drying sites. The English set up much of their inshore cod fishery on the Gaspé Peninsula, Placentia and Newfoundland's east coast. For six to eight weeks, crews loaded their double-ended rowing boats or shallops, and either sailed or rowed until they found cod. On both sides of the boats, the men dropped their single lines with hooks, usually baited with mackerel, just a couple of metres from the ocean bottom. Jiggling the fishing lines, an ancient technique, was enough to catch the cod, which were then heaved into the bottom of the boat. Fishers, starting with indigenous people, used primitive iron

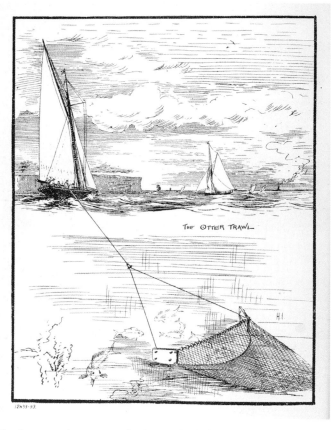

THE OTTER TRAWL

Trawl nets are the most productive method of catching cod, and the most threatening to the stocks and unwanted bycatch. Illustration from Lindsay G. Thompson, *History of the Fisheries of New South Wales* (1893).

hooks and lead weights on each hemp line. This centuries-old method, still used today in Norway with the spawning North-east Arctic stock and using nylon line, is called 'handlining'. Because of the abundance of cod, fishing techniques didn't change for centuries, lingering until the twentieth century. And why not? Returning to camp, each British team probably caught a thousand fish in a day or less. The abundance of fish was compelling and the work was very dangerous and strenuous.

Preparing salt cod was also tricky business. The more expensive premium-grade fish could be damaged at many stages – including during splitting, gutting and detaching the backbone; or salting (oversalting could burn the fish); or protecting the salted fish while drying when rainy or hot; or precise stacking in piles of up to 1,500 carcasses. Failure to salt the cod properly would result in a lesser grade, costing merchants much of their profit.

The premium salt cod that was shipped from the Banks controlled by the British allowed the Bristol merchants to expand their extensive salt cod market throughout the 1600s and to compete with those dealers dependent on cod from

Cod pots capture higher-quality cod with fewer injuries than other methods.

Iceland and Norway. The discovery of new cod fisheries also resulted in more consumption in Europe and the New World.

The cod fisheries of Norway and Iceland were quite different from those in the New World because of both the biological differences in the cod stocks and the climate. In Norway and Iceland, with the initial commercial fisheries, fishing was a winter affair with the cod coming to spawn in the cold winter darkness of the North. The winter fishing season allowed these fishers to be farmers in the summer. And the cold, dry weather in both Norway and Iceland made air-drying cod possible, producing stockfish. In the Newfoundland fishery and other North American fisheries, some cod came to the shore in the spring and summer chasing capelin, their foremost prey, while others were found in the Banks. Some New World fisheries could fish year-round because of the stocks that inhabited the shoreline.

Fishers in both countries, and other New World locations, employed methods that progressed from handlines to longlines (a line, possibly a mile long, to which shorter bits of line with baited hooks were attached) to gillnets and eventually the highly productive trawl fishing, with sock-shaped trawl nets dragged by the boat. In the late twentieth century, cod traps, invented in Labrador, were used only in Newfoundland and Labrador with migrating shore cod. With the present-day demand for better-quality cod, the cod 'pot' was developed, catching live fish with less bodily damage, as do hand and longlining. Whatever gear was used, it was vital to find the right spot for the best fishing.

In most of the New World, fishers had to use salt to preserve the fish because the climate was too wet and warm to only dry them. So they had to use a combination of both preservation techniques. This gave the French an advantage on the Banks because they had abundant salt, which they used to preserve the cod on the ship. As a result, they didn't have to land in Newfoundland to dry the cod, reducing the number of trips made annually from Europe.

There were distinct cures or varieties of salt cod. The French delivered the esteemed 'wet-cured' fish to their homeland markets – also called the 'green' cure, in which the cod were salted copiously and stacked in the ship's hold without drying them. The Spanish and other Mediterranean peoples didn't like the green cure, preferring lightly salted and dried cod, as most Europeans did. It also lasted longer in hot climates. For the English, salt was less plentiful and more costly, so they staked out the choice coastal locations in Newfoundland for drying (weather-permitting), building drying racks, or 'flakes', and consequently used less salt.

By the mid-seventeenth century, Newfoundland and Grand Banks salt cod, along with some other North American fish, had become a vital food source for hundreds of thousands of people. It was also a crucial commodity in the mushrooming economies of the North Atlantic colonies, and their commerce with Europe.

Northern New England Fishing

As the cod extravaganza continued to unfold in Newfoundland, the English and French also set sail south to the coast of Maine, which England claimed. This prolific fish was also being noticed further down the North American coast even when explorers weren't looking for it. Landing on the southern Maine coast in 1602, the English explorer Captain Bartholomew Gosnold was looking to trade with native peoples and for a possible settlement, and also searching for sassafras trees, a purported European syphilis treatment.

He chanced upon Native Americans – according to Brian Fagan, 'Micmac Indians dressed in European clothes rowing a Basque shallop', a coastal boat with oars and sails, obvious evidence of European influence. He continued south to the headlands that he renamed Cape Cod, later described by Henry David Thoreau in his essay 'Cape Cod' as 'the bared and bended arm of Massachusetts'. Here Gosnold observed huge quantities of cod.

Luckily, two adventurers on board made notes. One, the Anglican priest John Brereton, declared, 'We had pestered our ship so with Cod fish, that we threw numbers of them over-boord againe; and surely I am persuaded that in the months of March, April, and May there is upon this coast, better fishing and is as great plenty, as in New-found-land.' Another described mooring the ship in 'fifteene fadome, where wee tooke great store of Cod-fish, for which we altered the name and called it Cape Cod'. This area was also attractive because sassafras flourished nearby, the rocky coast was ideal for drying cod, salt might be produced close by in tidal pools and the fish were available almost year-round. And due to the warmer water, the fish were probably even larger than in Newfoundland, as much as or more than 45 kilograms (99 lb).

There were cod in intoxicating numbers in the Gulf of Maine, too. In 1614 the explorer Captain John Smith, like Gosnold, was struck by the vast quantity of cod and other fish off the coast of Maine, which he labelled 'New England'. He landed on Monhegan Island, Maine, the hub of local fishing for some British and French vessels. This was not Smith's first New World experience. He had been part of the 1607 colony in Jamestown, Virginia, whose boats fished in New England perhaps around 1608 to 1614. But once Smith realized the copper, gold and whales he wanted were non-existent, he turned to the local 'silver' at hand and directed his 37-man crew to land almost 50,000 *Gadus morhua*, using the livers to make lamp oil, which he brought back to England for a huge personal profit, along with 27 natives he sold into slavery in Spain. Meanwhile, with colonization in mind and as a proponent of this commercial cod fishery, Smith charted the Maine coastline down to Cape Cod, noticing the advantages of its many protected harbours compared to the coast of Newfoundland. Ever recruiting and, perhaps, mindful of the possible aversion to fishing, he promoted New England, 'Let not the meanness of the word *fish* distaste you, for [fishing] will afford as good gold as the mines of Guiana or Potosi, with less hazard and charge.'

Little did Smith or the colonists know that they were on the brink of finding another great fishery – the immense Gulf of Maine that extended from Cape Cod to Cable Sable, Nova Scotia, which contains the fecund Georges and Browns Banks. These banks, with an ideal environment for codfish, had shallow ledges protected by the banks and strong tides that mixed water from the sixty or so rivers that flowed into the banks. The bedrock of New England's commercial fishery has a coastline that is roughly 12,000 kilometres (7,460 mi.) long, and a surface area of approximately 93,200 square kilometres (36,000 sq. mi.), with an inshore fishing season in the winter.

Winter cod fishing sustained the fishers, safeguarding their cod fishing and trading stations along the New England coast for the first two decades of the seventeenth century. Fagan states that these were New England's original European maritime settlements that grew up alongside the Native Americans. For instance, by 1619 Monhegan Island had a significant prosperous fishing community that fished throughout the year. Excavations at a Monhegan fishing station uncovered typical cod-fishing gear of that era – a fishing spear, a gaff (a pole with a sharp hook to hoist a cod into the boat), fish hooks and lead sinkers to weigh down the fishing line. From Monhegan to the Charles River (whose mouth became the site of Boston), there were about ten makeshift fishing stations by 1620. In a decade, many of New England's major fishing ports were established, including Gloucester, Salem, Marblehead, Boston and Fall River.

Another was Plymouth. The credit for the first European settlement in New England officially goes to the Plymouth Plantation colonists who, in 1620, landed on the southern Massachusetts shore of this vast Gulf – initially with the intent to fish. English settlers also came for religious freedom, and Kurlansky argues that they came ill-prepared for fishing – lacking fishing gear, knowledge (they brought the wrong fish hooks) and wilderness survival skills. There were fish aplenty. Edward Winslow, one of the *Mayflower* leaders, acquaints us with Plymouth's splendid fishing grounds, 'Skote, Cod, Turbot, and Herring wee have tasted of; abundance of Musles the greatest & best that ever we saw; Crabs and Lobsters, in their time infinite.' This abundance made it a good location to build the first recognized settlement. The first three years were extremely difficult, and even farming, not their expertise either, was a flop until they discovered codfish fertilizer. Although stealing the hidden food caches of Native Americans sustained them at times, during the first year the indigenous people taught them how to hunt, find edible plants and eat clams and eels. Two years later, the Pilgrims were still desperate and begged for dried cod from the fishing stations on the Gulf of Maine.

Perhaps finding food wasn't just a lack of skill – some British were ambivalent about seafood, having eaten unappealing, sometimes spoiled fish from their home markets. Worse, it was also associated with compulsory religious 'fysshe dayes'.

In the early years in New England history, immigrants thought fish was insubstantial food, boring and unsatisfying, according to Sandra L. Oliver, author of *Saltwater Foodways*. Also, fishing was not work that the English settlers wanted as their primary occupation – it wasn't esteemed enough. They wanted to be farmers.

New England Native Americans in the 1600s ate many of the over eighty kinds of fish, including cod and shellfish, that supplied them with sustenance and were valuable enough to be traded. They fished in freshwater lakes and rivers, and salt water too. The Wampanoag in particular fished in the ocean for cod, mackerel, pollock, bluefish and others. They could have easily used their birch bark dugout canoes to catch cod near shore – shooting an arrow or using spears, gaffs and dip nets (a long-handled hand net) in more navigable shallow water. Native Americans also used hooks, local hemp line and nets. Gill nets hung vertically in the water with weights on the bottom and floaters at the top. Fish were caught in the net by their gills when they tried to swim through them. Fish could be cooked over or on the coals of fires; some were smoked.

Although colonists were still struggling to feed themselves, in the Gulf of Maine European fishers were doing stunningly well. English fishers from Plymouth, England, such as Emmanuel Altham, substantiated the bounty of cod fishing in 1623, writing that it was 'beyond belief'. His vessel fished off Plymouth, Massachusetts, and Altham wrote to his brother: 'In one hour we got 100 great cod . . . I think we got 1,000 in all.' He continued, 'One fish we got, I think, weighed 100 pound, it was as big a cod as ever was seen.' And many of the fishing boats they encountered, by Altham's account, went to Spain 'to sell their fish where they have ready gold for it'. Smith could have told them that, too.

In 1623 Governor William Bradford in Plymouth grumbled about being able to offer visitors 'a lobster or piece of fish without bread or anything else but a cup of fair spring water'. Other than fish, food was scarce from the start in New England.

Governor John Winthrop of the Massachusetts Bay Colony might agree with Bradford's gripe about the lack of good food. He came in 1630, part of that first wave of settlers, landing in Salem but travelling south to establish the second important settlement in New England – Boston. His complaint was that dried fish, clams and mussels were the only sustenance for families in the local towns. Dried fish was dried cod, a familiar staple shipped from Iceland to England, and eaten unenthusiastically during Lent. It was worth grousing about given the rigorous effort it took to make it palatable; some even used a kitchen stockfish hammer. In a fourteenth-century Parisian guide to domestic economy, the anonymous author wrote, 'it behooves to beat it with a wooden hammer for a full hour, and then set it to soak in warm water for a full two hours or more, then cook and scour it very well like beef; then eat it with mustard or soaked in butter.'

Twenty thousand Puritan immigrants swept over the emerging New England colonies from 1630 to 1640. Commercial fishing companies took advantage of the settlers, the majority of whom were poor and countless were dodging religious persecution. The dreamers of a lucrative fishing industry now had the means to make it happen – more access to local labour. The climate, bountiful inshore fishing in both summer and winter, and hungry markets in the Mediterranean and Spain worked in their favour. Eventually, New Englanders' aversion to fish declined and would turn to delight, if not rapture. Indeed, in 1769 succotash was included on the menu of the Founders' Day celebration in Plymouth. Succotash was an eastern Native American dish made of corn and beans, as well as fish and other ingredients different to those we use today.

Slave Trade and Cod

Another easier market opened up in the late 1640s for New England's salt cod. 'Refuse cod', or badly cured cod, was good enough to feed the starving enslaved Africans in the West Indian sugarcane industry, providing the necessary protein and salt to help survive on a Caribbean plantation. And at the right price, according to Keith Staveley and Kathleen Fitzgerald's *America's Founding Food*, 'two thirds of the price of top-grade goods', making this market one of the most important in New England's growing fishing industry. Prior to the opening of this market, refuse cod, possibly 50 per cent of every catch, was usually just tossed out.

Fitz Henry Lane, *Schooner Loo Choo in a Calm Sea*, 1850, oil on canvas. Invented in Gloucester, Massachusetts, in 1713, the swift and nimble American schooner was ideal for transporting salt fish or enslaved people.

M. J. Burns, 'Lost in the fog on the banks of Newfoundland',
in *Harper's Weekly*, 22 November 1879. Dory boats were launched
from a mother ship or from the shore and were easily lost in fog
or bad weather.

Kurlansky reports that over three hundred ships departed
Boston en route to the West Indies in the early 1700s. In 1713
Andrew Robinson, a shipbuilder from Gloucester, Massachusetts, invented a revolutionary new two-masted sailboat called
a schooner that was faster, sleeker and more manoeuvrable
than existing sailboats. It was effective for delivering salt fish
and transporting slaves, as well as fishing on the Banks and
coastal trading. Just before the American Revolution in 1775,
fish were New England's largest export, with salted meat in
second place. During the eighteenth century, New England
had matured into a powerful international cod dealer, and the
schooner was North America's most valuable vessel. Other
countries provided food for the slaves too. Newfoundland,
which produced different grades of salt fish, and even more
so Nova Scotia, whose speciality was refuse cod, also were
involved in this business.

J. Wrigley Publisher, 27 Chatham Street. N. Y

ONE OF THE CODFISH ARISTOCRACY.

In vain you try to make a show,
  'Mongst the proud flesh of cod-fish row,
Your home should be fast to a rod,
  Upon the banks of old Cape "Cod."

New England families whose wealth derived from *Gadus morhua* were called the codfish aristocracy, sometimes derisively.

Though the English who settled in the colonies wanted to farm more than fish, they eventually realized that the real treasure was the codfish, not ploughing the stony New England fields. A popular boat found in local fishing towns was the dory, also used for centuries in Europe. This small, flat-bottomed, sharp-bowed boat was rowed or sailed in either coastal or ocean waters. The fishing industry flourished in the coastal towns on the Gulf of Maine and the taste for fish blossomed. New England families who made fortunes from cod were the social elite, nicknamed, sometimes derisively, the 'codfish aristocracy'. The commercial fishing industry was so important that the image of a codfish was displayed in

In New England, cod was a symbol of wealth and prosperity. The 'Sacred Cod', a carved wooden effigy, has hung prominently in the Massachusetts State House since the early 1700s.

Fishermen had to risk their lives in all kinds of weather. Charles Napier Hemy, *Along Shore Fishermen*, 1890, oil on canvas.

various ways – on the seals of the Plymouth Land Company and the state of New Hampshire, on a shield on the *Salem Gazette* newspaper, and on various American coins. But the most prominent, symbolic and long-lasting of all is the almost 1.5-metre (5 ft) 'Sacred Cod', a white pine carving that hangs in the Massachusetts State House in Boston representing economic prosperity.

What was not acknowledged was the human price that was paid for this sacred fish. Gloucester alone has lost about 10,000 fishermen since it was founded in 1623. For a taste of their lives, dip into Rudyard Kipling's *Captains Courageous*, a tale about a pampered teenager who falls off a transatlantic steamship, is rescued by a Portuguese fisherman on a fishing schooner, and learns the hard way about the cod fishery off the Grand Banks of Newfoundland.

Cod Wars

Quarrels broke out over the precious cod, regardless of its abundance. Iceland, first settled in the ninth century by the Norse, was involved in many of the disputes, but not always as the instigator. It was one of the most bountiful fishing grounds on the way to the New World. As early as 1350, Iceland's dried cod became its principal export during a period of high demand for fish from Europe's Hanseatic League and the Christian Church. The Hanse's Bergen location controlled the Icelandic trade, selling this lower quality stockfish in Europe as a second choice to the superior Lofoten, Norway cure. By the early 1400s, England's Bristol merchants had initiated trade with both Iceland and Greenland, also bursting with additional marine resources. These competitors – the Hanseatic League, the Danish–Norwegian alliance and the Bristol merchants – incited the first of the 'cod wars', according to Rose, involving 'English fleets and seizures of ships by the Danish'. These many disagreements were officially designated as the Cod Wars in the mid-twentieth century.

Instead of soldiers and artillery, the ensuing skirmishes featured trawlers and gunboats. The main players were the United Kingdom and Iceland, and the issue was fishing rights for cod. The high seas were still considered free and open, but, in a gutsy move, Iceland created fishing limits around each of its islands.

After Iceland gained its independence in 1944, it seized even more control over its shorelines. It raised the ante in 1950 by extending the limit to 4 nautical miles. The notion that the ocean belonged to everyone was continuing to change. Jockeying for fishing grounds was common but it escalated into the official Cod Wars in the mid-1900s. Once more, Britain was at the centre of the clashes with Iceland in the North

Atlantic. There were three official Cod Wars over almost a twenty-year period, 1958–76. Luckily these disputes ended with only one official death and no war proclamations.

While economic pressures in Iceland and Britain were strong, humans were beginning to realize that this highly prized food source was not inexhaustible. Because of Iceland's stern determination, its fishery limits leapt from 3 nautical miles to 200 in less than 75 years. Eventually, the 200-mile nautical limit became a NATO standard and the Cod Wars ended.

The discovery of a new Asian spice route uncovered an unexpected ocean treasure in the form of this bountiful white fish. This led to a four-century expansion of the search for cod that created both wealth and conflict. There was also an

Detail of the map of Iceland from *Carta Marina* by Olaus Magnus, 1539, which portrays a cod on a shield, similar to the later coat of arms (which was the emblem of Iceland until 1903).

exponential increase in the availability of this valuable source of protein and in the demand for cod. Cod was now a regular part of the diet of people around the world. And while the citizens in these very different cultures all became cod eaters, they each developed their own intriguing methods for preparing the versatile *Gadus morhua*.

4
Trade Carries Cod Across the Globe, 1400–1970

Southern Nigerians love stockfish. But they didn't come by that love easily. During the Nigerian Civil War fifty years ago, many of the over 1 million civilians who perished died of starvation, particularly children. Heart-rending photographs of the skeletal survivors spurred worldwide relief efforts that came to their aid during this horrific crisis. Norway's donation was ideal: dried cod, or stockfish, that required no refrigeration and is chock-full of essential nutrients.

Today, stockfish is a major part of the Nigerian diet and central to Nigeria's culinary culture. All economic and social classes feast on it -- heads and tails for the poor, chunks and fillets for the better off. *Okporoko*, or stockfish, is enjoyed especially by the Igbo people in southeastern Nigeria. The name stems from the dull 'clunk!' sound of the rock-hard fish as it hits the pot. *Ugba* and *okporoko*, a stew, is considered a delicacy, containing stockfish, fermented oil bean seeds and habanero pepper, an extremely hot chilli pepper, among other ingredients. The unexpected pepper may have arrived in Africa with the Portuguese or possibly the Spanish – but both countries took chilli peppers to India and Southeast Asia. The Nigerian economy, with the largest population in Africa, continues to devour a sizeable part of Norway's stockfish exports. But Nigerians are not the only ones on the continent who developed a taste for dried cod. Many other Africans, particularly West Africans, enjoy stockfish. Nigeria is an example of how *Gadus morhua* became an important food source in a completely unexpected location nowhere near its native waters.

Cod became a global fish appearing on the plates of people from almost everywhere but Antarctica long before aircraft delivered fish far from their habitat. Starting in the fifteenth century, when the huge stocks were being discovered and harvested in the North Atlantic, the culinary trail of salt cod was being blazed by the Portuguese from Africa to India to Asia. They were in search of an ocean spice route, an alternative to the costly land route, that led from western Europe to the Spice Islands in Indonesia. This chapter also introduces the variety of preparations of fresh, dried (stockfish) and salted cod that were created along the Portuguese spice route, whether by the Portuguese themselves or by the people the

Ugba and *okporoko* is one of the most popular dishes in the Igbo area of Nigeria.

Portuguese encountered. Then we follow this fascinating fish to the rest of the world, including the New World, Europe, Scandinavia and Russia. Let's begin by retracing the voyages of the Portuguese explorers.

Portugal Spreads Salt Cod

The first to circumnavigate the globe and establish colonies and trading posts as they went, the Portuguese also created new culinary traditions in Africa, Asia and South America. Favourite Portuguese food, such as salt cod or *bacalhau*, became one of the many legacies of the European Age of Discovery, which lasted from the early fifteenth century to the mid-seventeenth century, a period of expansive overseas exploration.

The Portuguese were the principal European explorers and built trading partnerships around the world. Uncomfortably wedged between the Atlantic Ocean and Spain, they wanted to be the first to find a water route to the Spice Islands to capitalize on the prosperous spice trade. Improved technology, such as navigation tools to calculate latitude and the small manoeuvrable ocean-going caravel vessel, gave them the means. Conquering Ceuta, an affluent Islamic trading centre on the North African coast, earned them the first puzzle piece of the embryonic Portuguese empire. This maritime superpower's expansion lasted almost six centuries, from the Ceuta conquest in 1415 until 1999, when they surrendered the last colony, Macau, to China.

Whatever motivated the Portuguese to pursue trade and conquer new lands, they were nourished by their bounty of North Atlantic salt cod and generously introduced its culinary versatility along the way. After Ceuta, they continued their exploration of Africa while also discovering the Azores, Madeira and Cape Verde, archipelagos in the Atlantic Ocean west of Africa. In 1498, Vasco da Gama reached Calicut, India, opening up the trade route even further. Stores on da Gama's flagship, *São Gabriel*, were intended to last for three years. According to a 1551 historian's report, his fleet included a 200-ton supply ship plus three other vessels. Even fast days were observed with nutritionally rich codfish, rice or cheese replacing meat. Salt cod, ship's biscuits and meat were also part of a sailor's main diet.

Just two years later, Brazil was claimed by another Portuguese explorer, Pedro Álvares Cabral, opening South America to Europeans. Subsequent expeditions led to attempts to establish outposts and colonize the coasts of Africa, North America (including the Caribbean Islands) and Asia, and Portugal was the first European power to reach Japan.

The Portuguese are the most passionate about salt cod and endearingly call it *fiel amigo*, or loyal friend. It is considered their national dish and is an important cultural hallmark. But it was the Celts, who came to northern Portugal in the first millennium BCE, bringing their meat-salting skills with them, who enabled the Portuguese, who had enough salt to sell to the rest of Europe, to apply these techniques to fish. Their North Atlantic fish is salted and then partially dried to a water content of about 40 per cent. People of all classes consume this preserved fish, which they find at their favourite salt cod boutique, as do the Spanish. They choose from the large assortment varying in quality and colour (from frosty white to creamy) and guillotined to just the right size. For the Portuguese, cod has always meant salt cod. In both the Portuguese and Spanish languages, salt and fresh cod have the same name, *bacalhau* and *bacalao* respectively. Seldom is *bacalhau fresco* available in Portugal.

Some Portuguese claim that there are enough Portuguese salt cod recipes for every day of the year; others say there are more than a thousand. Regardless, there are favourites. Perhaps one of the most well known is the chickpea and salt cod salad, *salada de grão de bico com bacalhau*, served with crusty bread and crisp greens and washed down with Vinho Verde. A handful of other prized preparations include the beloved codfish cakes (*bolinhos de bacalhau*); fritters (*pastéis de bacalhau*); comforting scrambled eggs and potatoes with shredded salt cod (*bacalhau à brás*); casserole of salt cod, boiled potatoes and onions (*bacalhau à Gomes de Sá*); hearty salt cod stew (*bacalhau estufado*); and salted cod with cream (*bacalhau com nata*). Cream sauces dress up salt cod wherever it is eaten. Christmas Eve dinner often warrants *bacalhau de Consoula*, an unpretentious dish of salt cod, cabbage, hard-boiled eggs and potatoes.

One might expect to find some of these cod dishes in any of the Portuguese ports along its spice trade routes from West Africa to Southeast Asia. Many of these have been adapted by the local population with their own ingredients to suit their culinary traditions.

Colonization is a rough way to get introduced to new edibles. Yet some delectable, unimaginable combinations were created with local foods and new food items introduced by the colonizers. The Portuguese, who were setting up new outposts for provisioning their spice route search, were especially instrumental in introducing new plants and foods, and liberally shared their enthusiasm for salt cod. In contemporary Africa, many of these mash-ups are considered essential to the local diet. Take Angola and Mozambique, for instance, from where these foods spread to the rest of the African continent. These countries are on different African coasts and dissimilar geographically, but were the sites of Portuguese bases established in the late fifteenth century. Imagine the

Bacalhau à brás is a much-loved Portuguese dish of scrambled eggs, potatoes and shredded salt cod.

new flavoursome provisions arriving from the New World – cassava (manioc), chillies, maize, potatoes, sweet potatoes, sweet peppers and tomatoes. The Portuguese also brought chickens and pigs whose meat was mixed with native ingredients such as beans, pulses, sorghum and okra. One of the most popular dishes that has survived in Angola is *esparregados de bacalhao*, which marries salt cod with Angolan ingredients like cassava leaves, guinea pepper and sweet peppers, plus native African sesame or palm oil. Mozambique and other African colonies received luxuries from the East – citrus and other tropical fruits, varieties of beans and rice, many spices and sugar. These were gathered by the Portuguese from their exotic outposts on India's west coast, the Spice Islands in Indonesia, and Macau in South China.

Goa in India is another culinary melting pot with Portuguese, Muslim and Hindu influences. For more than 450 years, Goa, captured in 1510, was a portal to Portugal's eastern colonies. The exploding East–West trade was channelled through Goa, on the Indian west coast north of Calicut, where Vasco de Gama landed in 1498, the first European to find the sea route to Asia. By the mid-fifteenth century, Portugal had acquired two other Indian territories, Daman and Diu, that added to the trade route infrastructure.

The Portuguese brought New World foodstuffs, including chilli peppers (Goans adore them), guavas, pineapples and tomatoes, to the enormous population of India. Goans are

The Portuguese use salt cod in many recipes, like this *bacalhau à Gomes de Sá.*

seafood lovers and blended the Portuguese salt cod with their own recipes. Cookbook author Maria Teresa Menezes, in *The Essential Goa Cookbook* (2000), wrote of the Goans, 'A lot of people in Goa still get misty-eyed over *bacalhau* or Portuguese salt cod.' They prepared it with dried beans, such as the much-loved Portuguese chickpea, also with rice and salt-fish pickle, an accompaniment to rice and curry. Salt cod was fried in *fofos*, akin to the pervasive fritters, a version of which is found in almost all national cuisines. Goans also eat a Portuguese-Indian (Luso-Indian) codfish chutney as a main dish, rather than as the usual curry complement, according to another Goan cookbook author, Jennifer Fernandes.

There were other exchanges too. It is likely the Portuguese, who salted native fish, making the flavour much like salt cod, offered better salt-preserving methods for a local fish, *bombil*. The esteemed vindaloo is a union of Portuguese and Goan cuisine, found worldwide in Indian restaurants.

Macau, a Portuguese trading post for over four centuries, is also heavily influenced by Portuguese cuisine. Traditional Macanese cooking is hard to find since it is being nudged out by the new glitzy Michelin-starred restaurants for gamblers. But when one can find traditional cuisine, it still reflects a cross between Portuguese and Chinese, with a splash of East African, Indian and Malay. A remnant of the Portuguese spice trade, this cuisine has been relegated primarily to the home cook, a Macanese senior centre and an occasional restaurant. Riquexó, owned by an ethnic Macanese couple, still serves four *bacalhau* courses: *bacalhau à brás*, *bacalhau à lagareiro*, *bacalhau assado* and *cozido de bacalhau*.

Cod in the New World

At the same time as the Portuguese were sailing east to Asia, they also joined other Europeans who risked sailing west across a very large, uncharted ocean in search of better fishing. As we have seen, discovering cod from the North Atlantic was an unexpected windfall beyond belief.

Their westward voyages led to another part of the Atlantic Ocean: the Portuguese landed in what is now Brazil in 1500 and established this most important colony. But they were not successful in establishing colonies elsewhere in the New World.

In addition to their cuisine, the Portuguese brought another import. More than 3 million enslaved Africans were brought to toil on the sugar plantations established by the Portuguese, who also introduced salt cod, almonds, dried shrimp, garlic, olives and onions to Brazil. And with the Africans came their own foodways.

In Brazil, one pot meals are ubiquitous. Variations to the centuries-old Brazilian stew *moqueca de peixe*, from Bahia's mid-eastern coast, reflect the incorporation of ingredients from both the Portuguese and the Africans. An African method of wrapping stewed ingredients in leaves was transformed into *moqueca de peixe*, a stew in a great pot with coconut milk, palm oil (from West Africa), fresh coriander, garlic, red and green peppers, tomatoes and onions, often combined with salt cod pieces or perhaps shrimp or whatever fish is available, all served over white rice with *farinha* (manioc flour) sprinkled on top. The palm oil and *farinha* add flavour to the stew. It is genuinely a melting pot of cultures. The ever popular codfish fritters, especially in Brazil's capital of Brasilia, are frequently eaten as snacks, but mostly eaten before a meal, along with a beer.

As well as in Brazil, salt cod was consumed on many of the West Indies islands, where it is called salt fish. It was likely introduced by early Portuguese explorers, perhaps from one of Christopher Columbus's ships. The African slave trade is in part responsible for the varying foodways in this area; a brisk business in providing cheap food for enslaved people developed during this time. Remnants of low-quality salt fish can be found throughout the area, including at roadside stands, where various salt-fish fritters are served. Typically eaten immediately, at their tastiest, fritters are deep-fried batter with the addition of fish, fruit, meat or vegetable.

In the islands, salt fish comes in many forms. In Guadeloupe and Martinique there are the *acrats de morue*. Trinidad has *accras* and Puerto Rico has *bacalaitos*. In Barbados, fried codfish cakes are popular. Ackee, the West African fruit, combined with salt fish, usually cod, is considered Jamaica's national

Cod fritters are common in many cultures and deep-fried in anything from peanut oil to beef dripping.

dish, and is eaten for both breakfast and dinner. Treated as a vegetable, ackee can be sautéed with salt cod, onions, Scotch bonnet peppers, spices and tomatoes. A Jamaican salt-fish fritter, stamp and go, serves as party and breakfast food.

Since the first temporary fishing settlements were established in the New World, cod preparations have evolved from simple boiling or cooking over the fire to more elaborate renditions. Pan-fried codfish cakes from the Canadian Maritimes 'are as old as fisheries', writes Fagan. They are found in many provinces including Newfoundland and Labrador, requiring only fish scraps or leftovers and a starch. Dressing up either salt or fresh cod as a cake or patty calls for potatoes, eggs, flour, savoury seasonings such as onions, and cooking in oil or pork fatback. Each version of this far-reaching dish reflects the need for variety, thriftiness and adjustment to local ingredients.

A traditional Newfoundland rural dish is made with salt cod. Fish and brewis starts with a brewis (soaked hard tack or hard bread in water, dripping or fat), adding salt, and sometimes onions and salt pork, whose small fried cubes, or 'scruncheons', are scattered over the top. Root vegetables might accompany this well-liked meal. During the First World War, the 'Fish and Brewis' Fund was created to provide this 'delicacy' to the Newfoundland Regiment hunkered down in the French trenches. Both the sea biscuit, a long-lasting, twice-baked unleavened bread, and salt cod arrived, but without the salt pork. Newfoundlanders felt the troops would be longing for this comfort food.

Across the North Atlantic from Newfoundland, Icelanders have always been fond of fresh cod heads, which were also dried and eventually polished off as snacks. The dried cods' heads were so popular that they were transported inland on ponies. The skin and bones didn't escape the Icelanders'

Iceland exports its cod heads too.

ingenuity, either – they roasted the skin and boiled the bones into a porridge.

Icelanders were not the only ones who ate codfish heads. In 1747, in *The Art of Cookery Made Plain and Easy*, Britain's Hannah Glasse offered several ways to prepare a cod's head – roasting, boiling or baking – and grilled or fricasséed cod sounds (or swim bladder) with butter and mustard or with gravy. This was her first cookbook and became a bestseller. (Fish and chips had not yet met each other.)

Cod found a way into literature in the USA and the UK. Cod heads appear in Herman Melville's 1851 novel *Moby-Dick*, where on Nantucket, an island off the coast of Massachusetts, Ishmael, the main character, reports that the cows were fed on 'fish remnants', and they walked on the sandy beach 'with each foot in a cod's decapitated head, looking very slip-shod'. That explained the 'fishy flavor to the milk'. In 1856, another famous Massachusetts author, Henry David Thoreau, in his essay 'Cape Cod', wrote that the cows on nearby Cape Cod were also 'sometimes fed cod's-head'. These literary references are an indication of how European settlers, but not Native Americans, used cod as cattle feed and fertilizer.

In the mid-1800s, some Americans served a cod's head and shoulders as a centrepiece entrée popular on upper-class dinner tables. A 13- to 23-kilogram (30 to 50 lb) cod, which may have been over a metre (3 ft) long, was so large that the tender cod cheeks might have been the size of grapefruits, according to Sandra L. Oliver. This genteel presentation was accompanied by a sauce made with anchovies or shellfish.

Cod was sustenance for many North Americans, often as chowder. Also published in 1851, *The House of the Seven Gables*, by novelist Nathaniel Hawthorne, recounted that, 'A cod-fish, of sixty pounds, caught in the bay, had been dissolved into the rich liquid of a chowder.' Cod chowder was served for breakfast, dinner and supper on Nantucket in Melville's novel. The chowder scene featured two seamen ordering supper at a local hotel, 'and in good time a fine cod-chowder was placed before us' by the cook Mrs Hussey, who 'wore a polished necklace of codfish vertebra'. Cod as sustenance; cod as jewellery; eventually cod as wealth. Cod built New England and fed the fishers and the populace.

Sarah Orne Jewett highlighted the importance of an onion in chowder in the novella *The Country of the Pointed Firs*, a coastal Maine story. Mrs Todd, a local landlady, invited her Bostonian guest and narrator to a nearby island to visit her mother. They arrived with an onion. No wonder Mrs Todd's mother was so excited – it adds a flavour like no other, an essential ingredient to many chowders. It was common to fry the salt pork, removing it before adding a layer of fish, crackers, onions, potatoes tossed with the salt pork and, finally, fish. Fill the pot with enough water mixed with flour to cover it. This recipe can be found in the 1832 edition of *The American*

Frugal Housewife by Lydia Maria Child, a famous American writer and social activist. The layering technique is also seen in the first chowder directions that were published as early as 1751 in the *Boston Evening Post*.

Fish chowders or stews have been made for centuries by coastal inhabitants. They might have originated from any of the various nationalities in the fishery, but most likely French cooks. In the 1500s to 1600s, chowder was eaten in Brittany's fishing villages and migrated to the shores of the New World and other European countries.

The origin of the word 'chowder' is not clear, but some speculate that it is of French origin, from *chaudière*, or pot, and *la chaudrée*, or fishermen's stew. Chowder is well known in fishing villages from Brittany to Bordeaux. The cauldron held fresh fish and unleavened bread or savoury biscuit, plus some savoury flavourings. Perhaps this practice was brought by the Breton fishers to North America, where it became a favourite in the Canadian Maritime Provinces and New England and is now a main dish. In America, chowder parties or picnics held on the beach became very popular in the mid-1800s. Regardless of its origin, chowder was easy to make and the ingredients were usually at hand whether on a ship or in the cupboard of seaside dwellers.

Cod in Europe

Britain's famous fish and chips meal matches fresh cod fillet, deep-fried in batter, with fried potato, usually accompanied by malt vinegar and salt, and all wrapped in paper. British fish and chips is similar to America's hot dog in a bun – a quick, cheap snack or meal at the seaside or football game. There are regional variations in whether cod or haddock is

Fish and chips is England's and Scotland's national dish; either beef dripping, lard or vegetable oil is traditionally used to fry the fish. Historically, cod is the preferred fish for fish and chips in Lancashire, in contrast to Yorkshire, where haddock is the traditional choice.

preferred, or which fat for frying the fish is used – either beef dripping, pork lard or vegetable oil. Popular in the mid-nineteenth century with working-class families, fish and chips might be called England's national dish. And Scotland's, too.

The pairing appears to originate in the 1860s, perhaps in London or Lancashire. Historians are uncertain as to when exactly fish and chips were first served together. The two foods were available separately for more than fifty years before that. Fried fish could be purchased in cold pieces, as a common London street food, perhaps earlier than 1840, from roughly three hundred sellers. A 'fried fish warehouse' is mentioned in Charles Dickens's serialized novel *Oliver Twist* (1837–9), when fish was sold with a wedge of bread. The 'husky chips of potato, fried with some reluctant drops of oil' come later in his *A Tale of Two Cities* (1859). Fish fried with raw potato chips appears in French cookbooks as early as 1795. They may have originated with late 1700s street food vendors who sold the French fry and other cooked foods.

Cold fried fish might not appeal to many, but there is a Jewish tradition of fish fried in a batter eaten cold. In 1786 Thomas Jefferson stumbled upon 'fried fish in the Jewish fashion' during his only visit to London. Credited as the oldest fish and chip shop in London's East End still in business, Malin's of Bow was founded in the 1860s by Joseph Malin, a Jewish immigrant from Eastern Europe. This melding of immigrant cultures – the fish of the Eastern European Jews with the potato of the Irish, via the New World – created a fusion food symbolic of British cuisine. Fish and chips spread to Ireland and Scotland, among many other countries.

For over 2,000 years, fish has been consumed on many Catholic holidays that require abstinence from meat. Historically, these holidays have numbered over a hundred per year. For many of those years, fish was not popular and required

'Cod is a favourite of chefs due to its firm, dense flake and slightly sweet flavor,' according to Wulf's Fish of Boston, Massachusetts.

camouflage to make it more palatable. On the Continent, cod preparation in France progressed from a Lenten white fish pie to salt cod cloaked in such disguises as the famous béchamel cream sauce or secluded in a baked gratin. Pies were a common way to dress up seafood and a Savoyard master chef's 1420s recipe, from his cookbook, *Du fait de cuisine*, was said to please his employer, the Duke of Savoy, Amadeus VIII. Cream sauces were another method to conceal the flavour of fish, especially the harshness of salt cod. The first printed recipe for *brandade de morue* appears in a Nîmes cookbook, *Le Cuisinier Durand* by chef Charles Durand. A favourite of Nîmes, it is created with poached fish that has olive oil and milk fiercely beaten into it, producing a mush. Sometimes garlic and potatoes are added too, though the latter are not used in the south of France. Elizabeth David, distinguished British cookery expert, called this dish, 'Another triumph of Provençal cooking, designed to abate the rigours of the Friday fast'.

The Spanish also have a version, *brandada de bacalao*. Cod is ubiquitous in Spanish and Basque cookery – from salted to sautéed to smoked. As with Portugal, the mastery of salting protein arrived in northern Spain with the Celts, at about roughly the same time. Both the Portuguese and Spanish explorers of the New World brought back exotic ingredients such as cacao, corn, potatoes, tomatoes and chilli peppers. But salt cod is predominant in Basque kitchens thanks to early North Atlantic cod-fishing adventures. Those New World peppers are evident in some traditional Basque recipes: a salt cod stew, *bacalao a la vizcaína* (tomato and dried-pepper sauce), *bacalao al pil pil* (local red Espelette peppers) and *bacalao al club ranero*. Salt cod is served in countryside Basque cider houses and as sophisticated tapas or *pintxo*, especially in San Sebastian. The Basques are also fond of bread soup with salt cod, as are the neighbouring Portuguese.

A stockfish main course in the Ligurian style of northwestern Italy.

Croatian cuisine has been heavily influenced by neighbouring Venice, which occupied mostly Roman Catholic Croatia for almost four centuries. For instance, many northern Italians and Croatians like stockfish (*stoccafisso* and *baccalà* or *bakalar* respectively). Italians in Vicenza preferred a traditional stockfish preparation called *baccalà alla vicentina*, once popular in taverns and famous restaurants. Stockfish has been in demand in several Italian regions, where it is used in local dishes. It has even been celebrated by festivals in some Italian towns. Both Italy and Croatia import salt cod, too. Croatians are fond of salt cod in winter, particularly for special dinners during the Christmas season.

Cod is the undisputed king of fish in Norway. Edvard Grieg, Norway's most famous composer, reputedly said, 'My music seems to have a taste of cod in it.' Norwegians, having caught them since the Stone Age, of course have recipes for everything from fresh cod to cod that is dried, salted (or both), smoked and even soaked in lye. Norwegians love fresh cod best, but consume it in many other, often unusual, ways.

Concocted in Scandinavia as early as the 1500s, *lutefisk*, or lyefish, is a distinctive preparation of stockfish (and sometimes salt cod too) that is eaten in winter. After being soaked in a lye solution and rinsed thoroughly in running water, *lutefisk* is boiled, giving it a jelly-like consistency. It is usually served with melted butter, pepper, boiled potatoes and flatbread, though there are geographical variations. It can also be baked, poached, braised or steamed. Some Norwegians, Swedes, Finns in the Swedish-speaking part of Finland and their North American emigrant communities are fond of it, but for anyone else it is definitely an acquired taste.

Soaking in lye is a harsh treatment of stockfish. Davidson offers some reasons for the method: more water can penetrate

Invented in the 16th century, *lutefisk* is usually a winter preparation of stockfish that has been soaked in lye.

the rock-hard stockfish after being softened by the lye, and it worked well in cold Nordic climates before refrigeration. Some speculate that it could have been part of the cleaning process of stockfish after unsanitary transportation during the Middle Ages. Really, it is anyone's guess. While it remains beloved by many North American immigrants, especially as a part of age-old Scandinavian Christmas celebrations, its popularity is declining with them and in Scandinavia.

Large amounts of stockfish and klipfish, salted and dried cod, continue to be important Norwegian products. There are many preparation techniques, including pummelling it until edible and eating it with butter, or poaching it. Either for celebrations or every day, the Danes make a hot fruit soup, *søssuppe*, with boiled cod and fruit, fruit juice, some oatmeal, sago or tapioca, lemon peel strips, prunes and raisins, along with a dusting of cinnamon. Norwegians smoke the cod's tail, *røkerump*, and bake it with butter, sour cream and fresh carrots. The Dutch also have a recipe for a fresh cod's tail, *gestoofde kabeljauwstaart*, baked with butter, lemon and a bouillon, dusted with breadcrumbs and served with a side of boiled potatoes and carrots. After sampling these recipes, you may better understand why Nordic cuisine has changed so much. Although these recipes are still in use, their popularity has declined.

Cod roe, considered a caviar substitute, is harvested from female fish. It is now quite expensive, but prior to fishing quotas was quite reasonable. Roe can be boiled, fried or smoked, and served with a rich sauce, with lemon and potatoes. Davidson described a Flemish method of boiling a big muslin-wrapped cod's roe in salt water, which was poured out, allowed to cool and carved into slabs large enough to fry. The final product was devoured on bread or toast. Cod roe waffles, or *rognvafler*, are an unexpected way to enjoy this mashed, raw delicacy in parts of Norway. A Greek favourite is the smoked cod roe spread, pale pink *taramosalata*, originally made with the dried roe of the grey mullet. Recipes vary but might include a starchy base of soaked white bread or mashed potatoes, mixed with lemon juice, olive oil and a bit of thinly diced onion.

Many fishers rate the head, throat muscles or 'tongues' and cheeks as the finest or choicest parts of the cod, stresses Davidson. Add cod sounds, or air bladders, to the list as well. He mentions that in Norway the Bergen method involves baking cod tongues like a gratin with a white sauce, adding eggs and grated cheese. Salt cod sounds are baked in a pie in Newfoundland with salt pork, hard bread, raisins, molasses and spices such as cinnamon and cloves – a version of the traditional British 'mincemeat' pie. The Belgians make a dish, *kaasjes en keeltjes*, where the tongues and cheeks are taken out of tasty cod heads and then boiled with onions, salt, pepper and a splash of vinegar. Again, they're served with boiled potatoes and melted butter. The remaining heads are used for soup. Icelanders fry the sounds, and poach the throat muscles, serving them with the ubiquitous boiled potatoes.

Further east, the Barents Sea is home to one of the largest and most robust cod stocks in the world. Russians on the Barents Sea coast are very fond of their fish, and in Russia's south the phrase 'little fish' is a term of affection. Elena Ivan-ovna Molokhovets, in *A Gift to Young Housewives*, heaps considerable praise on the codfish in her fish recipes. This homemaker's guide is composed of almost seven hundred pages full of housekeeping tips and more than 3,000 recipes. Roughly 29 editions of this classic Russian domestic manual were printed, starting in 1861 and ending in 1917 with the start of the Bolshevik Revolution. It is a treasured tome that has been carted into exile, handed down through generations and

Fishmarket display of cod delicacies – roe and tongues – in Bergen, Norway.

peddled on Moscow's streets. Molokhovets recommends methods of preparing salt cod (soak for 24 hours) and stockfish including soaking, pounding and brining. She did admit that fresh cod is the tastiest. Her recipe for fresh or salt cod, cod with a cherry and red wine sauce, is an unusual and appealing combination of sweet and savoury. The cod is poached in milk and drained, then covered in a sauce of unsweetened cherry purée, butter, water or bouillon, red wine, sugar and spices (cinnamon and ground cloves), along with a little potato flour. Molokhovets also recommends cod with various sauces – potatoes and mustard, tomato, white table wine, and crayfish and morel sauce.

Who else but Norwegians would pair root vegetables and curry mayonnaise with a cod burger?

Cod cheeks, about the size of a large sea scallop, are one of the choicest parts of the cod.

'Life without fish is pretty much unthinkable for Russians,' writes Darra Goldstein, professor emerita of Russian and a culinary scholar. In her twenty-first-century Russian cookbook *Beyond the North Wind: Russia in Recipes and Lore*, she presents the results of her hunt for the heart of traditional Russian cuisine. Cod, according to Goldstein, is most beloved by northern Russians closest to where they're caught in the Barents Sea, and to a lesser degree further south. Northwest Russian citizens of Arkhangelsk, whose trawl fleet in the White Sea has sustainability certification, have been insultingly called 'cod-eaters', or country bumpkins.

Fresh cod is much loved in Russia and is found in fine grocery stores in Moscow, St Petersburg and other major cities. Goldstein describes Murmansk-style cod, a preparation of raw sushi-grade cod fillet that is seasoned with sea salt, pepper, a bay leaf and sunflower oil. Murmansk, a seaport in northwestern Russia with one of Europe's largest fish-processing plants, is north of the Arctic Circle near the Barents Sea, home of significant cod stocks. Goldstein offers a uniquely Russian version of baked fishcakes – it's a two-part process involving sautéing and then steaming cod in the oven. The garlic and dill are uncommon in Western fish cake recipes, as is the rye flour coating rather than breadcrumbs.

Braised cod with horseradish also calls for rye flour and dill. Goldstein reassures the reader that the heap of fresh horseradish (360 g, or 1½ cups), which steams along with the fish, does not vanquish the tender cod's flavour. Age-old Russian meals require hearty soups, including the prized fish soup *ukha*, a fisherman's soup long revered by both peasants and Francophile aristocrats. While there are territorial variations, Goldstein's recipe for Pomor-style fish soup mixes cod with salmon and halibut, replacing the traditional Pomor dash of fresh cod liver oil with more obtainable halibut cheeks, perhaps enhancing the flavour but reducing the soup's store of omega-3s. In Russia's far north, Pomors were the dwellers on the White Sea coast, and they would cook cod and halibut to create a clear fish broth.

Whatever cod's culinary transformation, it has been a critical food source in international trade, starting before the 1200s with the Norwegian stockfish. Cod fuelled the Viking rampages and explorations leading to the New World. Without the discovery of the huge stocks of codfish in the North Atlantic and their preservation by salting or drying, the Europeans, especially the Portuguese, may never have discovered the rest of the world so soon and the riches born of the ocean spice trade route. Cod not only fed sailing crews, but preserved cod became a staple in the diet of people who never fished for cod because it wasn't found in their waters or they were inland inhabitants.

Just as the Nigerians have integrated the Norwegian gift of cod with their native ingredients, other countries have transformed it into fast-food snacks, local daily fare, celebratory dinners, a substitute for meat for religious abstinence and more. The long culinary trail of the *Gadus morhua* demonstrates its enormous reach around most of the world's continents. Will this reach decline and this extraordinary fish disappear because of our voracious appetite? It had better not. Life without cod is pretty much unthinkable.

This trawler containing hundreds of thousands of codfish uses a giant net that is an example of the gear that makes overfishing so easy.

5
Sustainability in the Twenty-First Century

The incomparable cod fishery in Newfoundland collapsed in the early 1990s. The Canadian Minister of Fisheries and Oceans indefinitely closed this fabled five-hundred-year-old fishery that was the foundation of the Newfoundland and Labrador economy and culture. The abundant stocks had been destroyed, led close to extinction, primarily by international and Canadian overfishing. In turn, this ruling threw around 30,000 people out of work, shattering local fishing communities and costing the Canadian taxpayers billions of dollars. It also exposed the ineffective government regulations responsible for protecting the stocks, the impotence of cod scientists who sounded the alarm repeatedly, and the vulnerability of the fishers. How could this have happened?

For centuries, cod was a resource that we thought was inexhaustible. But when the number of cod has declined almost to the point of disappearing, as in this Canadian example, we've been hard pressed to recognize the severity soon enough. The pressure of growing world populations, with rising incomes, has increased demand. Also it's not easy to manage cod stocks, in part because it's very difficult to count fish. Plus, historically, technological advances have prompted new fishing methods, created better boats and engines, including steam and diesel, and developed such preservation methods as ice and refrigeration. All these advances have promoted overfishing, especially of the bigger breeding stock that produce the most eggs, and of bycatch, the marine life caught accidentally, including cod. Add to this list illegal fishing and governmental subsidies for those voracious industrial ships that dominate the high seas and overfishing is inevitable. For cod, according to Rose, the most destructive culprits are Portugal and Spain.

We're cocky, we humans. There have been declines of species before and we thought we could either revive them or do without them. But the ocean, which blankets two-thirds of the planet's surface, is a delicate ecosystem that isn't easily managed. Yet we have the means to increase the number of sustainable cod fisheries and preserve this iconic fish so humans can enjoy its delectable, delicate flavour rather than letting it become nothing but a memory. We have many options – from better-managed fisheries with catch limits, to

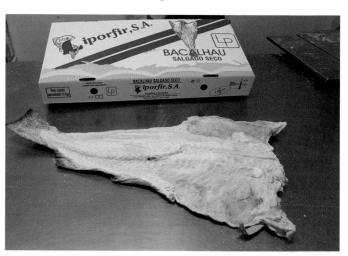

Fresh, frozen and salt cod from Iceland is shipped around the world.

Lofoten fisherman posing with a pair of enormous cod while standing on cod heads, 1910, photograph by Anders Beer Wilse.

no-fish zones, to smarter fishing methods, among others. This requires the fishing industry, governments, scientists and consumers to collaborate. These methods have produced results in the fisheries of Iceland, Norway and Russia, where the spawning stocks are 'in the hundreds of thousands to millions of tonnes', explains Rose. North American stocks obviously haven't done as well.

How to Count Fish

Almost thirty years later, the Canadian ban, which was intended to be temporary, is still mostly in place. There was a brief but stalled revival of Northern cod, but the fishery can't yet tolerate full-scale operation. If only humans could get an accurate idea of how many cod are in the ocean, it would make regulating the catch much easier. But it's hard to count all the codfish in the sea. We can record how many fish are brought into ports each year but that is only part of the story.

How do we determine how many cod to catch without devastating the stocks? Codfish stocks are regulated by governmental fisheries organizations created by countries' laws. Their fisheries scientists make estimates about the number of cod from many sources of information that help determine the condition of the stock, how productive it has been and what the limits of commercial fishing should be. Important data come from tracking the number of cod 'landings', that is, cod captured, brought into fishing ports and sold. ('Catch' is everything that comes up in the net out of the sea.)

Scientists also work on fishing boats to monitor catch samples, counting how many fish and other marine life are discarded (bycatch), and to get the fishers' opinions and data. In addition, scientific organizations own vessels equipped to survey fish and ocean conditions. Scientists try to calculate the size of a particular fish stock or total biomass – combining information about its age range, fecundity, spawning habits and natural and fishing mortality (from natural deaths and predation).

But these regulations and data do not always help. And we seem to have forgotten that we've exhausted cod once before in European waters. That was why the late fifteenth-century fishers sailed to the New World in search of more fish for a growing population after European fish and whale stocks were destroyed. But even in the New World there were concerns – as early as 1668, the Massachusetts Bay commercial cod fishery was closed for two months a year. W. Jeffrey Bolster, author of *The Mortal Sea*, guesstimates that the quantity of codfish in the Gulf of Maine today is less than 1 per cent of what it was just over two centuries ago. Will we ever see a

Codfish are deeply embedded in New England culture – this one is used on the sign of the iconic seafood restaurant chain Legal Sea Foods. It is missing the trailing barbel on its chin.

great storehouse of fish in the Northwest Atlantic again? Not if there's illegal fishing.

Counting fish is further complicated by illegal fishing by commercial fishermen who misreport their landings. 'The Codfather' is a startling example. Carlos Rafael, a Portuguese immigrant to the USA, known as 'North America's most notorious fishing criminal', engineered an enormous fishing fraud, discovered in 2017, that earned him his nickname. In New Bedford, Massachusetts, he was caught misreporting his ground fish catches of more than 318,000 kilograms (700,000 lb) as dabs, pollock and haddock, when they were really species that had stricter quotas, such as cod. Both he and his fishers paid a high price for this trickery – and with good reason. He was banned from fishing forever, fined and jailed.

The fishing industry works with governments and scientists to staunch the seemingly inescapable tide of cod stock destruction. Fishers are working with scientists to learn how the human-made sounds of offshore wind farms and shipping affect Atlantic cod spawning behaviour. But overfishing is the most obvious culprit. Certainly, there are other contributing factors: declining food sources due to ocean temperature warming; changes in the ecosystem and climate; and natural fluctuations in the stock. You can see it in the numbers – in three decades the huge cod biomass, which is the total weight of fish in a stock, was reduced from 'millions of tons to a small remnant of tens of thousands of tons', wrote Ray Hilborn, author of *Overfishing*, as early as 2012. But much of the devastation happened in the 1960s, when large foreign factory ships, trawlers that operated with such 'ruthless efficiency', as Bolster puts it, were largely responsible for destroying the Canadian fisheries.

But it's more than how many cod we catch. It's also about preserving large, older female fish. A 2018 *Science* article, 'Big Mamas Matter for Fish', described the story of how biologists studied over 342 fish worldwide and discovered that older female fish are the most productive. For over a century, humans have been aware that bigger fish with their larger ovaries produce more eggs. So what's new? Scientists have discovered their eggs are better – bigger and with more fat, which means more energy, ensuring the survival of more eggs – hence more fish. Researchers, who know the effect of size, call them BOFFFF – Big Old Fat Fecund Female Fish.

The problem is that the fishing industry, without even overfishing, has been harvesting the easy-to-catch larger cod. That means we're losing more of the breeding stock so fewer fish are produced to replenish it.

'We have become too skilled at fishing,' writes David Attenborough in his 2020 book, *A Life on Our Planet*. Even that may be an understatement. New, sometimes indiscriminate, use of technology has made almost every fish worth eating available for human consumption. We have come a long way from the simple hooks made from bones and natural fibre gillnets used by indigenous peoples.

It is often the case that technology developed during a major war can be quite handily adapted to another industry, such as the perfected diesel engine and electronics that pinpoint fish. By the 1960s, brawny trawlers had electronic navigation systems, radar and sonar, to target cod, developed during the Second World War. Many countries used them Great Britain, Japan, Portugal, the (then) Soviet Union and its satellite countries. This new technology had a huge impact on fisheries, enlarging fishing areas and allowing fishers to go to sea for an extended duration, six weeks for some factory ships. Although in the 1400s the Dutch had a version of factory ships, factory fishing was changed forever in the 1950s by the new super-trawlers. These gigantic factory ships are ocean-going vessels that process and freeze fish onboard. A freezing trawler can be as huge as 144 metres (472 ft) carrying 3,000 tons of fuel, processing 350 metric tons of fish a day, and can carry and stockpile 7,000 tons of processed fish. And they can also be the mother ship to a fleet of smaller vessels. In 2019 one of the world's largest factory ships could handle a breathtaking 547,000 tons of fish a year. We humans have certainly learned how to fish with merciless proficiency.

Changing Ocean Ecosystems

It was no contest for the cod. These trawlers were one of the main reasons for the collapse of the Canadian Northern cod fishery. The bottom trawlers damaged, some say destroyed, the ocean floor where cod live. The capelin fisheries using midwater trawls altered the cod's immediate ecosystem.

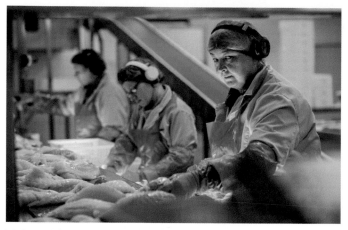

Today codfish are processed quickly and efficiently, sometimes on voracious factory ships.

A combination of many factors is undermining the eco-system. Ocean temperature warming because of climate change may make the water inhospitable for cod and reduce their food sources. Hilborn asserts that the growing carbon dioxide in the atmosphere creates a more acidic ocean, which could kill the food base. Climate change is certainly causing cod to move north for colder temperatures.

'Fishing changes ecosystems,' writes Hilborn. The sophis-ticated gear catches mind-boggling numbers of fish while sometimes damaging the sea floor. Overfishing and bycatch reshape ecosystems, upsetting the balance of predators and prey, which are also needed to feed the larger fish such as cod. Plus there is the reluctance of fishers, fishing communities and governments to limit or give up fisheries and a once profitable way of life.

It is logical that governments have become involved in managing cod stocks and setting fishing limits, as well as boundaries on fishing in nearby waters to safeguard fish resources for their countries and protect them from others. Of course, it's different for every country. The governments of the United States, Norway and Iceland have made a big difference. The USA has clarified what overfishing is and enacted rigorous laws to punish violators. It has also declared certain areas protected, where fish like cod can live without risk from fishers. Matching up the fishing fleet to the size of the local codfish stock stops the certain competition among fishers for available fish, which is what Iceland and Norway have done.

How to Rebuild

Preventing overfishing, specifically capping the number of cod caught, known as catch limits, is one of the main ways to rebuild stocks. Other methods include closing entire areas. As early as 1410 around Bergen, Norway, fisheries were temporarily closed to protect diminishing stocks. Also, adjusting

Racks of Icelandic salt cod waiting for packaging.

fishing gear can make a big difference – just raising nets to trawl higher above the sea floor allows cod to dive to avoid capture when a net closes in. Nets are dangerous because they catch the large, old, most productive female cod that don't bite while in the act of spawning.

How do we create sustainable fisheries? Hilborn defines sustainable fishing as reducing 'the abundance of fish to between 20 per cent and 50 per cent of what it was in pre-fishing times'. Even though there were some scientific surveys in the early 1900s, who really knows how many fish there were before humans began exploiting the fisheries? Perhaps a better definition of a sustainable fishery is one that is harvested or fished at a rate that doesn't shrink because of overfishing. Regardless, there has to be a baseline from which to judge whether cod are declining. Human memory is unreliable – each generation has a different idea about the normal numbers of cod. And when incorrect baselines are used in assessing cod stocks, they disguise long-term changes and increase the risk of overfishing and devastating the stock.

'The resilience of cod is truly astounding,' writes Rose. While we no longer have the great storehouse of cod we once had, overall cod stocks are not imperilled, though all fisheries have been overfished or poorly managed at some point. Some are thriving, such as the Barents Sea Northeast Arctic and Icelandic cod stocks, both of which have been hugely threatened by overfishing, illegal fishing and industrial development. (Norway and Russia divide the Barents Sea stock.) Both recovered with a quick response from management and some luck. In Norway, where there has been a successful spawning fishery of Northeast Arctic cod for a thousand years, gear restrictions are strict. Though Norwegian coastal stocks need restoring, some, like the Northern cod, are improving. Most of the European stocks were eventually rebuilt, becoming productive, but are still diminished. Others are seriously endangered, such as the stocks in Georges Bank, the Gulf of Maine and around Nova Scotia, which have been destroyed and are struggling to recover.

In 2017 the Icelandic stock was the biggest it's been since 1985, thanks to the country's sustainable fishery policy using catch quotas, 'and other sound measures, like spawning closure and closures of areas with too many juvenile fish . . . not to mention good surveys of cod's main food (capelin),' writes Rose. These measures have allowed Iceland, which has one of the greatest cod grounds, to catch the most fish while strengthening the stock. In Norway, the strict gear restrictions have really helped.

Humans have always thought marine life was limitless, particularly cod because they *seemed* inexhaustible. However, there

This cod tops the Institute of Contemporary Art (ICA) building in East Boston, a neighbourhood known historically as a port for shipbuilding and immigration.

is a tipping point between catching just the right number of fish balanced against their birth and death rates from natural mortality and predators. If overfished, like the Newfoundland cod fishery, the stocks can be so reduced that it is much more difficult and takes longer to restore. But catching the decline quickly and actively managing the stocks with closures, and balancing predators and prey, according to Rose, makes it possible to rebuild the stocks of this magnificent fish. Even from a minuscule remnant of an overexploited cod stock, they can come back. Meanwhile, we can support the sustainable fisheries and enjoy the many beautiful codfish that have been rejuvenated and are flourishing.

And no doubt this fish is worth saving. As the famous French chef Auguste Escoffier, in *Le Guide Culinaire* (translated in 1979 as *The Complete Guide to the Art of Modern Cookery*), said, if cod were more rare, 'It would be held in as high esteem as salmon; for when it is really fresh and of good quality, the delicacy and delicious flavour of its flesh admit of its ranking among the finest of fish.' It already is the 'finest of fish'.

6

Preserving, Buying and Preparing Cod

The Celts were no strangers to salt. They were one of the earliest tribes to extract sodium chloride from the 7,000-year-old underground Hallein Salt Mine near Salzburg, Austria. Salt has extremely useful characteristics – it's an essential nutrient for humans, an effective preservative and a desirable seasoning. It has also been a highly valuable trade commodity. The Celts were trading salt and more profitable salted foods extensively throughout Europe and beyond to North Africa and Turkey, using river systems for transport. But how did the idea of salting to preserve protein get from Hallein, literally meaning 'salt town', to the cod fishers on the Atlantic Ocean?

Conserving food to last through non-growing seasons has always been necessary for human survival. This chapter will describe the two most common methods of preserving cod – drying and salting – and how to prepare it for consumption. Both practices, while requiring different techniques, allowed fishers to take advantage of the bountiful cod stocks in the North Atlantic. In northern Europe, Norway had ideal cod-drying weather conditions. Iceland and the Faroe Islands were the only western North Atlantic countries with a similar environment for drying cod. Fishers in the North Atlantic from other European countries needed salt to preserve the cod for their long voyages home to their markets. Both methods require rehydration, which takes time and work in advance of preparation and cooking.

For centuries, cod was the most consumed fish in the Western world. It seemed to be an endless resource until recently. Now the consumer has to be concerned with preserving this precious resource. The distress is not unfounded, particularly with our history of stubbornly overfishing. Buying cod that comes from a sustainable fishery takes some attention, but not a lot of work, and supports the existing fisheries. But first, let's explore how cod was preserved.

Cod Preservation History – Dried and Salted

Humans have a long history of preserving fish. The Egyptians – the first to realize salt's preservation capabilities – generated a burgeoning trade in salted fish around 2800 BCE. Egyptians got salt from the Nile River marshes. Ancient peoples of the Italian peninsula figured it out too, even building their own Salt Road, *Via Salaria*.

Salting and drying were two of the earliest techniques of preserving vital protein. Salting began about 2000 BCE in China. Drying is much older, dating to 12,000 BCE. We know the Vikings dried cod and it may have begun even earlier in Norway, when settlers arrived around 11,000 years ago. Knowledge of these life-saving preservation methods took centuries to spread to the North Atlantic world of cod.

So who first stumbled upon the marriage of salt and cod? The origins are unclear. The salt-mining Celts may have been among the pioneers, given their sodium chloride trade. The innovative Celts – early Indo-European people who were scattered over much of Europe – knew their salt and used it to preserve meats. (That's why we enjoy the famous Parma ham and bresaola today.) As the Celtic warriors moved westwards, overrunning everyone starting around 400 BCE, they introduced their innovations as they went, including their knowledge of how to salt food. When the Roman campaigns ended around 50 BCE, remains of the migrating Celtic tribes were concentrated in secluded clusters on parts of the European Atlantic coasts, ranging from the British Isles to Brittany and to northwestern Iberia. With the transfer of their expertise at salting pork to the Romans, one could imagine those same skills were passed on wherever the Celts lived and applied to the protein at hand – in this case, fish.

As the Europeans' access to salt spread, they used it on a variety of fish, including herring and eels. The Hanseatic League, a northern European trading association, dominated the popular salted herring business, and traded salt (and stockfish) throughout the Baltic coasts. Salt was transported from the northern German saltworks in Lüneburg along the medieval Old Salt Route to the North Sea port of Lübeck. Portuguese salt, harvested after swamping low areas with ocean water and waiting for the water to evaporate, was in much demand for salting fish, and was exported to northern Europe, especially Britain, which also had its own salt springs, and to Holland, Denmark and others. From the Middle Ages until the nineteenth century, salt derived from evaporated sea water was the only kind that was good enough to use for preserving fish and meat. Once called bay salt, it is now known as sea salt, not to be confused with table salt. It has a first-rate flavour and is quite pure. Plus, the big crystals are desirable because they prevent 'salt burn', which hampers the curing action.

The Vikings had no local access to salt until they raided northern France, now Normandy, where there was plenty. Rose thinks it feasible that the Basques eventually learned of

The quality of salt cod has improved a lot since the early days.

the huge cod stocks from the Vikings, who led the Basques to the North Atlantic. The Basques, who salted whale meat and that of other marine species, have been gathering salt for at least 7,000 years. Beginning in the sixteenth century, Basque whalers used their salt on the cod from gigantic schools to supply their long voyages while scouring the oceans for more lucrative whales. If they brought back a new seafood to feed their hungry European market, so much the better. In the competitive international fishing environment, it would not have taken long for this new strategy for exploiting this plentiful resource to be shared and adopted. However the practice of salting cod began, it triggered a completely novel and profitable fish business. So, as in ancient alchemy, a common substance, fish, was transformed into something new – gold!

Until the nineteenth century, salting and drying were the only ways to preserve cod, and those methods made it a staple in diets in many parts of the world. The bulk of northern European countries did not have native salt, which was costly to acquire, so with a lot of wind and sun, drying was the obvious choice, especially for Norway, the Faroe Islands and Iceland. Dried cod – a protein slab that lasted five to seven years – was inexpensive to produce, easy to ship and simple to restore to an edible condition. Lacking the right environment, drying was not feasible for areas of southern Europe and most of the New World.

Salt cod was a godsend. Salting was not weather dependent and only required a reliable, affordable, good source of

Cod heads are a source of delicacies such as cheeks and tongues.

Site of the Hanseatic Museum in Bergen, which was a hub of European codfish trading for hundreds of years.

sodium chloride. Though it did require some care in curing, salt cod was faster and more convenient to produce than stockfish, and it tasted better and lasted longer. It was easy to transport and didn't spoil as quickly as other salted fish, such as herring and whale.

In the New World around the 1600s, cod commerce exploded with competitors trying to produce preserved cod throughout the year for expanding demand. That meant salt, which had become cheaper. And to prepare salt cod, the fish were typically salted and then dried. Once beheaded and gutted, cod were packed in barrels with layers of salt, which cut the water content by 60 per cent. Then, if possible, they were dried further to reduce the water content to about 40 per cent, ensuring a well-cured, desirable preserved codfish. Producers experimented with different versions. Sometimes cod were traded salted but not dried. These were known as 'green' cod, appearing in a more original condition than stockfish. Many French consumers, especially Parisians and those in the northern provinces, preferred the green cure, which meant cod could be caught and salted on the ship, which would then not have to land before returning chock-full to Europe.

The British preferred dried cod that had been sparingly salted, which safeguarded the salt supply, and for centuries this cure appealed to the Caribbean and Mediterranean markets. Both versions of salt cod were more desirable than stockfish but cost the consumer more. The British kept researching other cures – they concocted the Grand Banks 'summer-cured dried cod', called poor John, or Habardine. It is mentioned in Shakespeare's *The Tempest* when the king's jester describes a monstrous figure he discovered on the beach: 'A fish: he smells like a fish; a very ancient and fish-like smell; a kind of not of the newest Poor-John.'

Without standards for curing cod, the environment, supplies and catch goals dictated the quality. While fisheries strove to make the best possible salt cod, not all succeeded. Newfoundland had the most bounteous cod stocks. Coves along the Newfoundland northeast coast were the hub of a salt cod cottage industry, where families both fished nearby and then cured cod – gently salting and drying it on timber flakes in the windy, sunny, summertime weather. It was the best in the country. On the muggy south coast facing the Grand and St Pierre Banks, the salt cod couldn't compete on quality because of the hefty salting needed to endure the return voyage.

For Labrador, quantity was the target. The salt cod produced there was called the 'Labrador cure'; it was known for its poor quality. Eventually, along with some New Englanders and Newfoundlanders who wanted to salvage their flawed product, the lower-standard salt cod was shipped to the Caribbean to feed enslaved Africans and became known as the 'West India cure'. Nova Scotia especially concentrated on this below-par product.

Cheaper salt made it possible for stockfish-producing countries to produce salt cod as well. Eventually, salt curing (in addition to drying cod) was practised in Iceland, which began exporting salt cod in 1624, though not overtaking stockfish exports until the 1830s. In the late 1600s, Norway started salting cod. Not until the mid-1700s was salted cod, also called klipfish, of any significance in Norway; by 1800, it was about a quarter of its exports.

Stockfish is one of the most well-known products of drying – the oldest and easiest way to conserve many other foodstuffs besides fish worldwide. Once dried, stockfish can last for at least two years if properly stored. It maintains its nutrients and is highly transportable, perfect as a commodity and as provisions for exploration. 'Stockfish' is the English translation of the Norwegian *stokkfisk*, which is also called *torrfisk*, or dry fish. In *The Oxford Companion to Food*, it is also described as 'stick-like fish', which is not a surprise when you realize it is so hard that it has to be beaten with a stick to make it more pliable and then soaked before it can be consumed. Another explanation is that to dry cod in this manner, two gutted, beheaded cod are attached by the tails and draped on wooden racks, also called 'sticks' or poles (from the Dutch word *stok*, to dry).

Drying alone draws out enough water, reducing it by 85 per cent, to prevent the enzymes and micro-organisms in the water from destroying the cod. The race to dry food before it spoils depends on how fast it dries. Cod are ideal for drying because they have plenty of surface area (compared to their size), which translates into faster loss of water. Iceland, the Faroe Islands and Norway have the dry air and wind that accelerate drying. Drying does not work well for oily fish such as herring or salmon because they become rancid when their highly unsaturated oils are exposed to oxygen. Stockfish is

Salted and dried *klippfisk* near the city of Kristiansund, 1925, photograph by Anders Beer Wilse. Norwegians developed many methods of salting, drying and storing cod.

cured by a fermentation process that allows cold-adapted bacteria to mature the fish, a practice that is similar to ageing cheese and Parma ham. Icelanders continue to make stockfish; the dried heads are sent to Nigeria.

The stockfish made in the Lofoten archipelago of Norway, within the Arctic Circle, is unrivalled. This area has some of the most suitable conditions – a dry climate with little rain, plenty of wind, and a temperature that's a little above 0°c (32°F). The cod are hung on open-air timber racks by the tail for about three months, from February to May, when weather conditions guard against insects and bacteria, as well as the frost and ice that can damage the fish. The cod are then transferred to an indoor drying area for close to twelve months. After drying, the stockfish are sorted into over twenty categories, based on aroma, quality, size and thickness. Prime and second grade are most common. Look for a natural shape, a clean neck and belly, and no blemishes, dewing, mildew or frost. When cooked, some describe the taste as mild with a firm texture; others say it has a gamey flavour. Double check that it's real cod – other fish such as haddock, pollock (saithe) and tusk are dried too. Rose unabashedly declares that none is as good as cod.

Despite its many attributes, consumption of salt cod far exceeds that of stockfish and is the only form of cod many people consume. It is produced primarily in Norway, Iceland, the Faroe Islands, Canada and Russia.

Until the Norwegians tapped their vast oil and mineral resources, seafood exports were crucial to their economy. Seafood still plays a big role in Norway, which touts its rank as the second-largest seafood exporter in the world after China. Wild cod and farmed salmon represent the bulk of Norway's seafood exports. Today Norway claims to be the world's largest producer of both dried and the more popular salt cod, with 90 per cent made from the Northeast Arctic cod stock.

Once salt became available in the late 1600s, the Norwegians began making klipfish by salting it and then laying it on flat rocks near the ocean to dry. Today, their klipfish is dried indoors. They now prefer to prepare it by pickling rather than salting. The raw cod is salted with sea salt and then matures in a pickling solution of water and salt for ten to twenty days. Next, it is dried for two to seven days on pallets indoors in a special drying tunnel at 20 to 25°C (68–77°F) until it has a water content of 40 to 50 per cent, then refrigerated at zero to 5°C (41°F). The salting and drying combination increases the power of the saltwater solution to interrupt the enzyme and micro-organism action. Stored in the refrigerator, salt cod will last for up to eighteen months. Like stockfish, salted cod has two primary grades – first and second – and is then ranked by size. Both must be desalinated before preparing.

Iceland, another country with few natural resources, also relied on cod as the backbone of its economy. According to the Icelandic novelist and Nobel Laureate Halldór Laxness, in his novel *Salka Valka*, in Iceland, 'life is first and foremost salt fish but not dreams and fancy.' Cod has always been taken very seriously. At first dried cod was essential food at home until exporting started in the 1300s: 'cod was the money and

Icelanders have been air-drying cod for centuries, as in this photograph taken in Kirkjusandur, before 1898, by Sigfús Eymundsson.

haddock was the food,' says Björgvin Þór Björgvinsson, Business Iceland's head of seafood, about a country whose cod stocks are primarily exported. (Haddock continues to be preferred over cod, though more cod is being consumed.) Today, Iceland still controls some of the world's richest cod stocks, and its fresh cod market is most significant, at about 40 per cent of export value and growing, as is the global demand for fresh cod. In addition, the rest of the export value of Iceland's codfish is roughly 30 per cent frozen cod, 15 per cent or less salt cod, and about 7 per cent dried cod. The stockfish market has declined a lot since 1990.

Today, there is an industry trend to deliver more fresh and frozen spotless cod to consumers. If there are fewer codfish, then higher quality must be delivered. But it's not easy. Fishers must minimize the trauma when pulling cod out of the ocean: swiftly bleeding and cooling the fish improves the quality considerably. Cod pots developed by the Canadians to capture cod without injury are another method of producing more pristine cod. Once captured, the fish are rapidly bled and chilled. Hand- and longlining have reappeared in response to this demand. This is good news for cod lovers because Harold McGee, a food science author, in *On Food and Cooking* (2004), notes that cod on ice maintain their freshness for about five days. Both Norway and Iceland are noteworthy for their high-calibre cod and exacting sustainability standards that protect this cherished species.

How to Prepare Salt Cod and Dried Cod

Once the consumer purchases preserved cod, what next? Both stockfish and salt cod require soaking prior to cooking. While stockfish simply needs to be rehydrated, salt cod demands desalting. Some fishmongers will sell stockfish and salt cod pre-soaked and ready to cook. Regardless, buy the best quality of cod you can find. For salt cod, look for almost white fillets (rather than yellowish or reddish), as thick as 5 centimetres (2 in.) or more in the middle. They're often sold in wooden boxes cloaked in coarse salt.

Rehydrating stockfish requires immersing the dried fish in clean, cold water that is changed daily and kept refrigerated. It's possible to remove the skin while soaking it. Time ranges from two to four days for fish chunks to seven days for a whole cod. It will double its dried weight.

There are different opinions about the process of de-salinating salt cod. How long it's soaked or frequency of water changing will affect the salt content. Usually, the package will include directions. But here's one interpretation from David Leite, on Leite's Culinaria website:

To soak the cod, bathe it under the faucet to wash off any salt on the exterior. Put the salt cod into a large bowl or rectangular container covering it with two inches of cold water. Wrap the vessel tightly in plastic wrap and refrigerate it for 24 to 48 hours, changing the water three to four times daily. (For example, with .45 kilos or 1lb. of salted fish, use 1,420 ml or 6 cups cold water.) Empty the water from the bowl, gently remove the fish, and remove the excess water with a paper towel.

Sample it as you go, cautions Leite. Err on the less salty side, because it's an imprecise process, and it's impossible to remove salt once it's prepared and easy to add more later. The plumped-up fish is now ready to be cooked. If it's a whole fish, first remove the skin and bones. The cod is still raw and will spoil if not refrigerated or cooked right away.

A 1930s cigarette card, showing how cod has always been a popular choice at the fishmonger's.

'Gasp-inducing accolades' are what any cook will get from preparations of the 'thickest, firmest' specimens of salt cod, promises Leite, a Portuguese-American food writer and James Beard award winner. He's a fan of salt cod's 'complex and, curiously, almost sweet taste and incomparable texture'. He recommends you buy the Norwegian version in any Greek, Italian, Portuguese, Spanish or Latin American market.

Leite isn't the only fan of Norwegian klipfish. Many chefs love it because of its reputedly distinctive taste, versatility and flaky texture, with 'lovely pale flesh and uniform color', according to the understandably biased Norwegian Seafood Council (NSC), the country's seafood marketing association.

Fish, less nourishing than red meat, more appetizing than vegetables, are a compromise, a '*mezzo termine* which agrees with almost every temperament and which can even be permitted to invalids', wrote Jean Anthelme Brillat-Savarin in *The Physiology of Taste*, first published in France in 1825. Brillat-Savarin wasn't the only one to think that fish wasn't completely up to snuff.

But there is no quibbling today. Cod tastes good, and is good for you. Cod and other seafood are more flavoursome than freshwater fish and, some even claim, meat, because of the ocean environment. And any 'saltiness' produced by the ocean water is neutralized by cod's abundant amino acids. A nutritional superstar, *Gadus morhua* is in the top twenty protein sources in the world. A kilogram of preservative-free stockfish is said to have about the same amount of protein as 5 kilograms of fresh fish – what a boon for humans! What other fish can make that claim? Stockfish packs a lot of punch nutritionally, maintaining the minerals and vitamins of a fresh fish. It is known for retaining its lean protein, vitamins (A, B,

C, D and E) and multiple minerals, though lower in omega-3 fatty acids than some fattier fish.

Both fresh and salt cod have solid amounts of lean protein as well. One hundred grams of Norwegian salt cod has an appealing 17 grams of protein, a smattering of vitamins (including A, B, C and D), minerals (especially potassium) and some of the 'good fats' – omega-3s and a dash of omega-6s. For some, the lack of carbohydrates is a plus in this non-fatty fish with, a mere 315 kilojoules of energy (75 calories).

There are two fish contaminates associated with cod – the industrial toxin mercury, and parasites or cod worms. Fortunately, cod has a low mercury content, so is one of the safest fish to consume. Mercury usually collects in large predatory fish with longer life spans, and filter-feeding shellfish. The Environmental Defense Fund Seafood Selector maintains that humans can safely eat up to four servings of cod a month, excluding the consumption of other contaminated fish. Check your local sources for the most current information.

Cod do host parasites. Cod worms are round worms, and they can be harmful to humans if the fish is not cooked or properly frozen. They can cause symptoms such as a tickling in the throat and can penetrate the stomach or small intestine, resulting in pain, nausea and diarrhoea. They can be found in cod that is salted, cold-smoked, sushi or slightly marinated. However, they do not affect the nutritional value. Finding a cod worm in your fish may mean that the fishmonger or processor was careless, but all kinds of efforts have been made to intercept them before they get to the consumer. It just happens occasionally.

To neutralize the worms, McGee recommends either cooking fish to a minimum of 60°C (140°F) or freezing it. But the u.s. Food and Drug Administration (FDA) suggests a slightly higher internal temperature of 63°C (145°F). The flesh is done when the cod's delicate translucence is transformed into a milky white or opaque colour, and is flaky. At these cooking temperatures, watch cod carefully because it may dry out. For home cooks, freezing is unfeasible because freezers are rarely below -18°C (0.4°F), and the FDA advises freezing fish for fifteen hours at -35°C (-31°F) or -23°C (-10°F). A good alternative is to buy frozen cod.

The cod is also famous for another reason – its liver. Since perhaps even before the Vikings, a foul-tasting, nourishing oil has been made from the cod's liver. This pale yellow oil is mainly derived from *Gadus morhua*, along with some of its other Gadidae family members. For centuries, despite its strong fishy smell, cod liver oil has been used especially for rickets, and as a restorative, because it is rich in vitamins A and D, as well as omega-3 fatty acids. An early important commodity for Norway, along with stockfish, the oil was used in leather tanning, lamp oil, paint, soap and other commercial endeavours. It is still in use and available online in different flavours, and now produced in Iceland, Japan, Norway and Poland.

Norwegians tout their fresh cod, or *skrei*, as the best in the world. The NSC claims that white fish sales have climbed continuously for the last twenty years, which is all to the good for their fresh cod sales. This migrating stock from the Barents Sea is named after an old Norse word meaning 'wander'. Their premier product, 'Quality Labelled Skrei', which is just 13 per cent of fresh cod, is a seasonal delicacy, and is wild caught only – from February to April – from the pristine Norwegian waters during spawning season. It is processed within twelve hours of being caught. The NSC describes *skrei* as 'chunky and succulent', and most delicious if cooked to 38°C (100°F).

Fresh fish deteriorates more quickly than any other food – even chicken or beef. Meat's microbes and enzymes are

In the late 1800s, Scott's Emulsion was marketed as a more palatable version of cod liver oil in the Americas, Asia and Europe.

disabled in our home refrigerators – not so with cold-water fish. They contain enzymes and bacteria that are comfortable living in very cold water, just above freezing in the deepest water to about 21°C (70°F) in surface waters, and also in chilly fridges. Cold-water fish like cod are abundant in unsaturated fats but that also makes them more vulnerable to ruin by oxygen and, hence, decay. McGee recommends putting fresh fish in a bag of ice at the supermarket, then rewrapping it at home in watertight plastic, and immersing it in an ice-filled container that can be covered. Store it in the fridge's back corner and be sure to use it quickly.

How to Consume Cod Sustainably

Cod lovers want to ensure that this iconic and delicious big-flake fish endures. To that end, it is critical to avoid eating cod from depleted stocks or fisheries that don't use sustainable fishing methods. The Icelandic and Northeast Arctic stocks are in very good shape, and some Canadian stock are being harvested too. These sustainable fisheries need our business in order to survive.

There are many seafood watch programmes in the world that have developed apps to make it easy to search for the best and worst sources of u.s. and Canadian Atlantic Cod, including the Monterey Bay Aquarium's app, Seafood Watch. It also has a list of other global seafood-rating organizations, such as the uk's Marine Conservation Society's *Good Fish Guide*. Of course, you can always use Google to search 'seafood rating organizations' to find information about Atlantic cod available near you.

At some supermarkets, you can identify sustainable fish by the easily identifiable blue and white ecolabel on the fish package on more than 30,000 products and menus in over two hundred countries. This aid to consumers is from the non-profit independent Marine Stewardship Council (msc), which assesses and certifies everything from large industrial to artisanal sustainable global fisheries. Using independent certifiers, the msc determines whether the fish stock is healthy

The msc, a global organization, certifies that certain seafood, including cod, is sustainable. Look for the blue-and-white fish eco-label.

and long-lasting, whether the fishing activity diminishes the environmental footprint supporting a healthy ecosystem, and whether it is well managed. For consumers, the MSC helps check the status of individual cod fisheries on their 'Track a Fishery' webpage. Check it out before shopping for dinner.

It has become increasingly common for fish to be farmed. So where is Atlantic cod being farmed? Iceland has given it up. After previous failures due to many codfish escaping and slow cod growth, producers in Norway have restarted this method of large-scale breeding again. Norway, with its multi-billion-dollar salmon industry, is certainly the country to give it another try. However, salmon farming, for example, can be harmful to wild salmon stocks. Besides, it's hard to imagine anything better than fresh, wild-caught cod.

Given the rise in concern for the ethical treatment of our food sources, it's worth a brief mention about whether cod feel pain. Some research shows that fish do change their behaviour in response to possible painful experiences, leading more and more biologists to believe that fish do feel pain and stress, even though they do not have a cerebral cortex.

There is evidence that fish flesh is in better condition when the fish are killed humanely. While more expensive, the use of humane methods such as electrical stunning followed by a quick death are being used by at least one Seattle-based seafood company on Pacific cod. While fish welfare is more of an issue in aquaculture, watch for changing fishing practices as these approaches increase – they may instigate a revolution in the way wild-caught fish are treated. If we're willing to pay more for free-range eggs, will we do the same for the beloved Atlantic cod?

What does it mean to consumers to consume cod sustainably? It does not mean eating it sparingly. It does mean being cognizant of the origin of the codfish you're buying for dinner.

Since overfishing has been incredibly damaging, despite their resilience, we must support cod stocks that are managed sustainably and avoid those that are endangered. The countries that have, with the help of scientists, instituted strict limits and particular protection for spawning clusters and juveniles, along with the fishing industries and fishers that buttress them, deserve our help and our business. And whether you are buying fresh cod in New York, *bacalhau* in Lisbon, klipfish in Oslo or stockfish in Lagos, it is up to you, the consumer, to have the will to save the iconic cod.

Will cod continue as a human food source? Over 5 million years, the adaptable cod, native to the North Atlantic, became the supreme fish of all the gadoid family, thriving in an assortment of habitats ranging from coastal inlets to rich offshore banks. Some of these cod stocks have been solidly restored. Some still languish. But the potential is there for all the cod stocks to be rebuilt and continue to be one of the most protein-rich fish in the sea, available to cod lovers around the world. As preeminent scientist, and fan, George Rose writes, 'The Northern cod rebuilding . . . argues that even when reduced to a tiny fraction of historic abundance fish stock can come back (IF WE LET THEM).' So let's do our part to keep the cod and sustainable fisheries alive for centuries to come. Be like the Portuguese explorers and treat cod as your *fiel amigo*, or loyal friend. Buy and eat sustainable codfish.

Recipes

Historical Recipes

Pastés Norrois (Norwegian Pasties)
Unknown author, *Le Ménagier de Paris* (1393)

Norwegian Pasties be made of cod's liver and sometimes with fish minced therewith. And you must first parboil them for a little and then mince them and set them in little pasties the size of a three-penny piece, with fine powder thereon. And when the pastry-cook brings them not cooked in the oven, they be fried whole in oil and it is on a fish day . . .

To Bake a Cod's Head
Mrs Hannah Glasse, *The Art of Cookery Made Plain and Easy* (1747)

Butter the Pan you intend to bake it in, make your Head very clean, lay it in the Pan, put in a Bundle of Sweet Herbs, an Onion stuck with Cloves, three or four Blades of Mace, half a large Spoonful of black and white Pepper, a Nutmeg bruised, a quart of Water, a little Piece of Lemon-peel, and a little Piece of Horse-reddish. Flour your Head, grate a little Nutmeg over it, stick Pieces of Butter all over it, and throw Raspings [browned bread crumbs] all over that. Send it to the Oven to bake; when it is enough, take it out of that Dish, and lay it carefully into the Dish you intend

to serve it up in. Set the Dish over boiling Water, and cover it
with a Cover to keep it hot. In the mean time be quick, pour all
the Liquor out of the Dish it was baked in, into a Sauce-pan, set
on the Fire, to boil for three or four Minutes; then strain it, and
put to it a Gill of Red Wine, two Spoonfuls of Ketchup, a Pint
of Shrimps, half a Pint of Oysters, or Muscles, Liquor and all;
but first strain it, a Spoonful of Mushroom-pickle, a quarter of a
Pound of Butter rolled in Flour; stir it all together, till it is thick
and boils; then pour it into the Dish, have ready some Toast, cut
thus Δ and fry'd crisp. Stick Pieces about the Head and Mouth; lay
the rest around the Head. Garnish with Lemon notched, scraped
Horse-reddish, and Parsley crisped in a Plate before the Fire; lay
one Slice of Lemon on the Head, and serve it up hot.

Cod-Sounds Broiled with Gravy
Mrs Hannah Glasse, *The Art of Cookery Made Plain and Easy* (1747)

Scald them in hot Water, and rub them with Salt well; blanch
them, that is, take off all the black dirty Skin; then set them on
in cold Water, and let them simmer till they begin to be tender;
take them out and flour them, and broil them on the Gridiron; in
the mean time take a little good Gravy, a little Mustard, a little Bit
of Butter rolled in Flour, give it a boil, season it with Pepper and
Salt, lay the Sounds in your Dish, and pour the Sauce over them.

To Crimp Cod the Dutch Way
Mrs Hannah Glasse, *The Art of Cookery Made Plain and Easy* (1747)

Take a Gallon of Pump Water, and a Pound of Salt, and boil it
half an Hour, skim it well, cut your Cod into Slices; and when the
Salt and Water has boiled half an Hour, put in your Slices, two
Minutes is enough to boil them; then take them out, lay them on a
Sieve to drain, then flour them, and broil them. Make what Sauce
you please.

Fish Pie

Maria Eliza Ketelby Rundell, *A New System of Domestic Cookery* (1807)

Cod or Haddock, sprinkled with salt to give firmness, slice and
season with pepper and salt and place in a dish mixed with oysters.
Put the oyster liquor, a little broth, and a bit of flour and butter,
boiled together, in the dish cold. Put a paste over; and when it
comes from the oven, pour in some warm cream. If you please,
you may put parsley instead of oysters.

Chowder

Mrs Lydia Maria Child, *The American Frugal Housewife* (1832)

Four pounds of fish are enough to make a chowder for four or
five people; half a dozen slices of salt pork in the bottom of
the pot; hand it high, so that the pork may not burn; take it out
when done very brown; put in a layer of fish, cut in lengthwise
slices, then a layer formed of crackers, small or sliced onions, and
potatoes sliced as thin as a four-pence, mixed with pieces of pork
you have fried; then a layer of fish again, and so on. Six crackers
are enough. Strew a little salt and pepper over each layer; over the
whole pour a bowl-full of flour and water, enough to come up
even with the surface of what you have in the pot. A sliced lemon
adds to the flavor. A cup of tomato catsup is very excellent. Some
people put in a cup of beer. A few clams are a pleasant addition.
It should be covered so as to let a particle of steam escape, if
possible. Do not open it, except when nearly done, to taste if it
be well seasoned.

Salt Fish with Parsnips

Charles Elmé Francatelli, *A Plain Cookery Book for the Working Classes*
(1861)

Salt fish must always be well soaked in plenty of cold water the
whole of the night before it is required for the following day's

dinner. The salt fish must be put on to boil in plenty of cold water, without any salt, and when thoroughly done, should be well-drained free from any water, and placed on a dish with plenty of well-boiled parsnips. Some sauce may be poured over the fish, which is to be made as follows: viz. – Mix two ounces of butter with three ounces of flour, pepper and salt, a small glassful of vinegar, and a good half-pint of water. Stir this on the fire till it boils. A few hard-boiled eggs, chopped up and mixed in this sauce, would render the dish more acceptable.

Scalloped Cod

Fanny Farmer, *The Boston Cooking-School Cookbook* (1896)

Line a buttered baking-dish with cold flaked cod, sprinkle with salt and pepper, cover with a layer of oysters (first dipped in melted butter, seasoned with onion juice, lemon juice, and a few grains of cayenne, and then in cracker crumbs), add two tbsp oyster liquor, repeat, and cover with buttered cracker crumbs. Bake twenty minutes in hot oven. Serve with egg or Hollandaise sauce.

Creamed Salt Codfish

Fanny Farmer, *The Boston Cooking-School Cookbook* (1896)

Pick salt codfish in pieces, and soak in lukewarm water, the time depending upon hardness and saltiness of the fish. Drain, and add one cup Thin White Sauce. Add one beaten egg just before sending to table. Garnish with slices of hard-boiled eggs. Creamed Codfish is better made with cream slightly thickened in place of Thin White Sauce.

Brandade de morue
Adapted from Auguste Escoffier,
A Guide to Modern Cookery (1907)

Cut one lb of *morue* into pieces, and poach these for eight minutes. The eight minutes should be counted from the time the water begins to boil.

Drain on a sieve, and clear the pieces of all skin and bones. Heat in a sautépan one-sixth pint of oil until the latter smokes; throw the cleaned pieces of *morue* into the oil; add a piece of crushed garlic the size of a haricot-bean, and stir over a brisk fire with a wooden spoon until the *morue* is reduced to shreds.

Then take the saucepan off the fire, and, without ceasing to stir the paste, add thereto, little by little, as for a mayonnaise, about one-half pint of oil. When the paste begins to stiffen through the addition of the oil, now and again add a tablespoon of milk. For the amount of *morue* used, one-quarter pint of boiling milk should thus be added by degrees.

When the *Brandade* is finished, it should have the consistency of an ordinary potato purée.

When about to serve, taste the preparation and rectify its seasoning.

Dish the *Brandade* in a hot timbale, building it up in the shape of a pyramid, and set thereon a crown of bread-crumb triangles fried in butter just before dishing it up.

N.B. – The Triangles of fried bread may, with advantage, be replaced by lozenges made from puff-paste, which are baked without colouration. For the *Brandade* use only well-soaked Icelandic or Newfoundland *morue*.

Soufflée de morue
Auguste Escoffier, *A Guide to Modern Cookery* (1907)

Finely pound one-quarter lb of freshly poached and flaked *morue*, and add, little by little, two tbsp of hot and very thick Béchamel sauce. When the paste is very smooth, season it; put into a saucepan, heat it, and add the yolks of three eggs, and four whites beaten to a stiff froth.

Put the whole in to a buttered soufflé-saucepan, and cook after the manner of an ordinary soufflé. Take either Icelandic or Newfoundland *morue* for this dish.

Bacalao a la Vizcaína
Manuel María Puga y Parga, *La cocina práctica* (1915)

Once the *bacalao* is de-salted, it's cooked, then the skin and bones are separated out.

In a skillet with abundant oil, fry a piece of bread, breaking it up in a mortar and pestle when it's golden. In the same oil, fry a large quantity of onion cut into circles and a few garlic cloves. When the onion is tender, put the mixture in a cake pan, in which you incorporate the *bacalao* and the bread, seasoning it with sweet and hot pepper, saffron, and a pinch of cinnamon. Cook over low heat, and shake it a few times so that the fish will not stick to the bottom.

Cape Cod Turkey (Stuffed Codfish)
Adapted from Sheila Hibben, *The National Cookbook: A Kitchen Americana* (1932)

1 medium-sized codfish
4 slices salt pork
3 tbsp butter
⅓ cup (80 ml) soup stock
1½ tbsp dry vermouth
1 small onion
1 small celery stalk
1 cup (120 g) breadcrumbs
½ coffeespoon (¼ tsp) thyme
¼ coffeespoon (⅛ tbsp) sage

1 hard-boiled egg
salt and pepper

Prepare a freshly caught codfish; wipe well with a damp cloth, and rub inside and out with melted butter, salt and pepper. Reduce soup stock to ¼ cup, add dry vermouth. Melt 2 tbsp of butter in a saucepan, and add to it finely chopped onion and finely chopped celery. Before the onion and celery begin to brown, add coarsely rolled breadcrumbs and let brown a very little. Moisten with the combined soup stock and dry vermouth, and add thyme, sage, chopped hard-boiled egg, and season highly with salt and pepper. Stuff the fish with this mixture, and sew up the cavity. Lay the slices of salt pork in a baking-pan, and put the fish on top of them; dredge with salt and pepper and bake in moderate oven, basting frequently with the grease from the pork. Allow 15 minutes to each pound of fish, and when done serve on a hot platter with quartered lemon.

Treska s Sousom iz Vishen' i Krasnogo Vina (Cod with Cherry and Red Wine Sauce)
Elena Ivanovna Molokhovets, *A Gift to Young Housewives* (1861)

Cook the cod in milk as described in Cod with Tomato Sauce. [Soak fresh or freshly pickled (marinated, fermented) not too salty cod in water for two hours, wash, bring to boil twice, changing water, rinse with clean hot water, add boiled whole milk, barely covering the fish, and cook until ready.] Drain the milk, rinse with boiling water, drain again. Heat ¼ cup of cherry puree with one spoonful of butter, dilute with 1½ cups of water or broth, add some sugar (to your taste), 2 to 3 crushed cloves, a little cinnamon, a teaspoon of starch, diluted in one tablespoon of water, cook. Add ½ to 1 cup of red wine, bring to boil, pour over the cod.

Modern Recipes

Ackee and Saltfish
permission to reproduce granted by Dr Jessica B. Harris

4 servings
60 g (2 oz) boneless salted codfish
3 strips bacon, cut into 2.5 cm (1 in.) pieces
28 g (1 oz) butter
1 medium onion, chopped
6 cloves garlic, minced
2 medium tomatoes, chopped
500 g (16 oz) can Jamaican ackee
5 g (⅓ tsp) Jamaican pepper sauce, or to taste
Note: canned ackee is very fragile and should be gently
stirred with a fork.

Desalt the codfish by placing it in boiling water to cover and cook
for 5 minutes. Drain and cool under running water. Flake the fish
with your fingers and set aside. In a large skillet, fry the bacon
until crisp. Add the butter and heat until it foams slightly. Add the
onion and garlic and sauté until the onion is transparent. Add the
tomatoes and pepper sauce and continue to cook for five minutes.
Stir in the salt fish, cover, lower the heat, and cook for three minutes. Check flavour. Gently stir in the ackee, cover, and cook until
the ackee is cooked through and has absorbed the flavour. You
may need to add a bit of water to keep it from sticking. Serve hot.

Bacalhau à Brás
permission to reproduce granted by David Leite,
Leite's Culinaria, recipe posted 2003

1 lb (450 g) dried salt cod, soaked overnight and cooked
7 tbsp olive oil, divided
1½ lb (680 g) russet potatoes, peeled, cut into matchstick-size

strips (about 6 cups)
1 large onion, thinly sliced
1 bay leaf
8 large eggs
½ tsp salt
½ tsp freshly ground black pepper
4 tbsp chopped flat-leaf parsley leaves, divided
18 black or green olives

Flake the fish, discarding any bones. Heat 4 tbsp of the oil in a heavy, large nonstick skillet [frying pan] over medium-high heat. Add the potatoes in batches and sauté until crisp and golden, about 7 minutes per batch. Transfer the potatoes to paper towels to drain. Add 1 tbsp of the oil to the same skillet. Add the onion and bay leaf and sauté until golden, about 15 minutes. Discard the bay leaf. Reduce the heat to low. Add the remaining 2 tbsp oil to the onion slices in the skillet. Mix in the fish and potatoes. Whisk the eggs, the ½ tsp salt, and the ½ tsp pepper in a large bowl to blend. Add the egg mixture and 3 tbsp of the parsley to the fish mixture in the skillet. Cook over medium heat until the eggs are softly set, stirring occasionally, about 3 minutes. Transfer the eggs to a platter. Garnish with the olives and the remaining 1 tablespoon parsley.

Bacalhau à Gomes de Sá
permission to reproduce granted by David Leite, *Leite's Culinaria*, recipe posted 2018

olive oil
2 large Spanish onions, cut in half and then sliced into half-moons
2 bay leaves
4 garlic cloves, minced
salt and freshly ground pepper
1¾ lb (800 g) Yukon Gold potatoes, sliced 1 to 3 mm (1⁄16 to ⅛-in.) thick
1½ lb (680 g) salt cod, soaked and cooked

²/₃ cup (120 g) pitted Kalamata olives in oil, sliced, plus more
for garnish
6 large hard-boiled eggs, 4 eggs cut crosswise into
5 or 6 slices each; the remaining 2 eggs cut lengthwise
into quarters
2 tbsp chopped flat-leaf parsley

Position a rack in the middle of the oven and crank the heat to
175°C (350°F). Drizzle a good glug of the oil (maybe 3 to 4 tbsp)
in a large skillet [or frying pan] and set over medium-high heat.
When the oil shimmers, add the onion slices and bay leaves. Cook,
covered, stirring occasionally, until the onions are golden and soft,
20 to 25 minutes. Add the garlic and cook 1 minute more. Slide off
the heat and let cool slightly. Meanwhile, liberally coat a 2-quart
(approx. 2 litres) casserole dish with olive oil. Sprinkle the bottom
with salt and pepper. Line the bottom with some of the potato
slices, overlapping them in concentric circles, creating a flower pat
tern. Scatter some of the cooked onions and olives over the potatoes. Place some of the chunks of cooked salt cod on top of the
olives and potatoes. Top with one sliced hard-boiled egg. Cover
with a layer of potatoes and top with a good glug of olive oil and
a generous amount of salt and pepper. Continue layering the
onions and olives; salt cod; sliced egg; and potatoes, salt and pepper – ending with potatoes. Occasionally press down on the casserole to make sure the layers are even and flat. Cover the pan with
foil and slide it into the oven. Cook until the potatoes are tender
when pricked with a fork or skewer, 30 to 60 minutes, depending
how many layers you have. Uncover the casserole and continue
cooking until the top is lightly browned, about 10 minutes more.
Remove the pan from the oven and let the casserole cool slightly.
Strew the remaining olives, the parsley, and top with the egg quarters. Proudly carry the pot to the table and wish everyone bom
apetite!

Okporoko Soup

Adapted from Gladys Plummer, *The Ibo Cookery Book* (1947)

okporoko (stockfish)
1 bundle spinach
3 tbsp rapeseed (canola) or any neutral vegetable oil
ogili igala (fermented oil seeds)
salt to taste
1 large onion
2 large peppers

Wash and steep *okporoko* for five minutes. Boil water. Add oil, ground pepper and *ogili igala*. When soup is boiling add spinach and *okporoko*. Serve with pounded yam.

Lemon Pepper Crusted Cod

permission to reproduce granted by the Newfoundland and Labrador Department of Fisheries, Forestry and Agriculture

4 servings, main dish
4 tbsp mixed peppercorns, coarsely crushed
2 tbsp plain (all-purpose) flour
¼ tsp salt
four 170 g (6 oz) skinless cod fillets
1 garlic clove, crushed
1 tbsp Dijon mustard
juice and zest of 1 large lemon
3 tbsp olive oil
2 tbsp fresh coriander, chopped
salt and pepper

Mix peppercorns, flour and salt. Coat cod fillets in flour and peppercorn mix, pressing on both sides. Set aside. In a small bowl, make a sauce by whisking together garlic, mustard, lemon juice and zest, oil and coriander. Taste for salt and pepper. Set aside. Spray a large non-stick frying pan with non-fat cooking spray. Add fish and sauté over medium high heat for about 3 minutes per side, until golden. Remove fish to platter and keep warm. Pour sauce into the pan and cook for 2 minutes until it is reduced a little. Pour sauce over the fish. Serving suggestions: serve with roast potatoes and a green vegetable, or with a green salad.

Cod Cobbler

permission to reproduce granted by the Newfoundland and Labrador Department of Fisheries, Forestry and Agriculture

1 ½ lb (680 g) Atlantic Cod fillets
1 ½ cup (350 g) unsalted butter
⅓ cup (40 g) flour
2 cups (450 ml) whole milk
1 cup (120 g) cheddar cheese, grated

Biscuit Topping
½ cup (60 g) cheddar cheese, grated
4 tbsp unsalted butter
1 tsp baking powder
1 ¾ cup (210 g) flour
¼ tsp table salt
½ cup (115 ml) whole milk

Place cod fillets in the bottom of a greased 9 × 9-inch casserole dish. Make a cheese sauce by melting butter and adding flour, let cook for about 2–3 minutes, then gradually add milk, stirring constantly, until thickened, then add grated cheese and cook just until cheese is melted. Pour sauce over cod fillets. Make biscuits by sifting flour, salt and baking powder together and then rubbing in butter until mixture resembles coarse meal. Add grated cheddar. Mix milk and egg together and pour into flour mixture. Toss gently to form workable dough. Roll out onto lightly floured board and cut into circles with biscuit cutter. Place on top of cod and sauce mixture. Brush biscuits with a little milk and sprinkle with a little grated cheddar. Bake at 450 degrees (230°C) for 25–30 minutes.

Fish Taco
permission to reproduce granted by Business Iceland

Fish
200 g (7 oz) cod fillets
50 g (2 oz or 4 tbsp) garlic oil
chilli sauce

Batter
550 g (20 oz) beer
400 g (16 oz) flour
10 g (½ oz or 2¼ tsp) salt
10 g (½ oz or 2¼ tsp) baking soda

Coleslaw
50 g (1¾ oz) carrots, julienne
150 g (5 oz) white cabbage
150 g (5 oz) red cabbage
juice from 1 lime
4 g (or a pinch) salt
50 ml (1¾ fl. oz) apple cider vinegar
2 g (or a pinch) parsley

Chilli mayo
200 g (7 oz) mayonnaise
15 g (½ oz or 1 tbsp) chilli sauce (sriracha)

Other ingredients
tortillas 6″ (15 cm)
lime slices
finely chopped coriander leaves
1.5 l (1¾ pints) frying oil
spring onions

Simmer red cabbage, white cabbage and carrots in a pan. Add vinegar, lime juice and salt. Finish with parsley and remove from heat. Prepare the batter. Mix flour with baking soda, salt and beer and stir. Cut fish to approximately 5-centimetre (2 in.) strips. Rub with garlic oil and chilli sauce. Cover in batter and deep fry in oil at 180°C (350°F) for 5 minutes. Serve on a tortilla with coleslaw, chilli mayo, spring onions, coriander and a slice of lime.

New England Fish Chowder
permission to reproduce granted by Chef Jasper White, *50 Chowders: One-pot Meals – Clam, Corn and Beyond* (2000)

8 servings, main dish

4 oz (110 g) meaty salt pork, rind removed and cut into ⅓-inch (1 cm) dice

2 tbsp unsalted butter

2 medium onions (14 oz [400 g]), cut into ¾-inch (2 cm) dice

6 to 8 sprigs fresh summer savory or thyme, leaves removed and chopped (1 tbsp)

2 dried bay leaves

2 lb (900 g) Yukon Gold, Maine, PEI or other all-purpose potatoes, peeled and sliced ⅓-inch (1 cm) thick

5 cups (1.2 l) strong fish stock, traditional fish stock, chicken stock or water (as a last resort)

kosher or coarse sea salt and freshly ground pepper

3 lb (1,400 g) skinless haddock or cod fillets, preferably over 2 inch thick, pinbones removed

1½ cups (360 ml) heavy cream (or up to 2 cups if desired)

for garnish: 2 tbsp chopped fresh Italian parsley, 2 tbsp minced fresh chives

Heat a 4- to 6-quart [5–6 litre] heavy pot over low heat and add the diced salt pork. Once it has rendered a few tbsp of fat, increase the heat to medium and cook until the pork is a crisp golden brown. Use a slotted spoon to transfer the cracklings to a small ovenproof dish, leaving the fat in the pot, and reserve until later. Add the butter, onions, savory or thyme, and bay leaves to the pot and sauté, stirring occasionally with a wooden spoon, for about 8 minutes, until the onions are softened but not browned. Add the potatoes and stock. If the stock doesn't cover the potatoes, add just enough water to cover them. Turn up the heat and bring to a boil, cover, and cook the potatoes vigorously for about 10 minutes, until they are soft on the outside but still firm in the centre. If the stock hasn't thickened lightly, smash a few of the potato slices against the side of the pot and cook for a minute or two longer to release their starch. Reduce the heat to low and season assertively with salt and pepper (you want to almost over season the chowder at this point to avoid having to stir it much once the fish is added). Add the fish fillets and cook over low heat for 5 minutes, then remove the pot from the heat and allow the chowder to sit for 10 minutes (the fish will finish cooking during this time). Gently stir in the cream and taste for salt and pepper. If you are not serving the chowder within the hour, let it cool a bit, then refrigerate; cover the chowder *after* it has chilled completely. Otherwise, let it sit for up to an hour at room temperature, allowing the flavors to meld. When ready to serve, reheat the chowder over low heat; don't let it boil. Warm the cracklings in a low oven (200°F [90°C]) for a few minutes. Use a slotted spoon to mound the chunks of fish, the onions, and potatoes in the centre of large soup plates or shallow bowls, and ladle the creamy broth around. Scatter the cracklings over the individual servings and finish each with a sprinkling of chopped parsley and minced chives.

President's Birthday *Plokkfiskur* (Icelandic Fish Stew)
Chef Margrét Thorlacius (Iceland President Guðni Thorlacius
Jóhannesson's mother), permission to reproduce granted
by Business Iceland

600 g (20 oz) cod or haddock fillets
1 medium-size onion
500 g (18 oz) potatoes
3 tbsp flour
50 g (2 oz or 4 tbsp) butter
approximately 300 ml (½ pint) fish broth
salt and coarse pepper

Bring water to a boil and then add the cod fillets to the boiling water. Lower the heat significantly and leave the cod in the pot with a lid for approximately 10 minutes. Cut the onion into small pieces. Peel and boil the potatoes. Now take the fish from the pot and place on a dish. In a saucepan, sauté the onions in the butter and stir in the flour to make a roux. Then add the fish stock and stir until the texture is like a beautiful pudding. Lower the heat, flake the cod and roughly chop the potatoes, and then stir them together with the sauce. Add salt and pepper to taste. Serve with fresh rye bread and plenty of butter and enjoy!

Stoccafisso Accomodato alla Ligure
permission to reproduce granted by the Norwegian Seafood Council

4 servings, main dish
2 tbsp extra virgin olive oil
1 garlic clove
50 g (2 oz) pine nuts
100 g (3 ½ oz) olives (some recipes say green olives, others mention both green and black olives)
2 anchovies in oil
1 red onion, finely chopped
1 carrot, finely chopped
1 celery stalk, finely chopped
600 g (21 oz) soaked and cleaned stockfish
½ glass (75 ml/2½ oz) white wine
400 ml (¾ pint) tomato puree or sauce (some recipes also include some canned tomatoes in sauce)
500 g (18 oz) potatoes
salt and pepper

Heat the olive oil in a pot or casserole. Add the garlic clove (peel away the skin but leave the cloves whole), pine nuts, olives and anchovies and pan fry. In the meantime, finely chop the celery, carrot and onion, and add these to the pot. Remove the fishbones from the stockfish and cut it into portions. Add the fish to the pot. Add the white wine and let it evaporate over a lively flame, it should take approximately 10 minutes. Once all the alcohol from the wine has evaporated, add the tomato puree and stir. Peel the potatoes, cut them into chunks, and add them to the pot. Cover the ingredients with water and season with salt and pepper. Cover the pot with its lid and leave to cook over a moderate flame for approximately 1 hour 30 minutes, then serve.

Stoccafisso di Norvegia Dorato
permission to reproduce granted by the Norwegian Seafood Council

4 servings, appetizer
2–3 tbsp extra virgin olive oil
wheat flour to cover the fish
800 g (28 oz) rehydrated, cleaned and dried cod
2 cloves garlic
1 handful of capers
150 g (5 oz) black olives
500 g (18 oz) cherry tomatoes, halved
salt and pepper
fresh basil

Cut the stockfish into chunks, flour it and fry it in the oil. In a saucepan place the garlic, a few tbsp of olive oil, capers, olives and halved tomatoes. Cook for 5 or 6 minutes and season with salt and pepper. Add the basil and serve with a green salad.

Traditional *Lutefisk*
permission to reproduce granted by the Norwegian Seafood Council

4 servings, main dish
2 kg (4½ lb) *lutefisk* (previously soaked, steeped in lye solution and rinsed)
200 g (7 oz) bacon
2 tbsp salt

Pea stew
11 oz (300 ml) dried yellow peas
1 tsp butter
salt
sugar

Preheat the oven to 200°C (400°F). Cut the *lutefisk* into servings and place in a baking pan with skin side down. Sprinkle with salt and cover with aluminium foil or a lid. Bake the *lutefisk* in the oven for approximately 30 minutes. Smaller amounts of *lutefisk* require shorter time in the oven. Dice bacon and fry on medium heat so the fat melts and the bacon becomes crispy. Pea stew: Leave the peas in water over night. Cook them in fresh water until tender and the stew evens, approx. 45 minutes. Add more water if it gets too firm. Gently add butter and taste with salt and a little sugar, to taste.

Serve the *lutefisk* with bacon, pea stew and almond potatoes.

Select Bibliography

Attenborough, David, *A Life on Our Planet* (New York, 2020)

Bertelsen, Reidar, 'A North-East Atlantic Perspective', *Acta Archaeologica*, 61 (1991), pp. 22–8

—, 'Gruel, Ale, Bread, and Fish: Changes in the Material Culture Related to Food Production in the North Atlantic 800–1300 AD', Publications from the National Museum, *Studies in Archaeology and History*, XXVI (2018), pp. 107–18

Boileau, Janet P., 'A Culinary History of the Portuguese Eurasians: The Origins of Luso-Asian Cuisine in the Sixteenth and Seventeenth Centuries', PhD dissertation, University of Adelaide, 2010

Bolster, W. Jeffrey, *The Mortal Sea: Fishing the Atlantic in the Age of the Sail* (Cambridge, MA, 2012)

Child, Lydia Maria, *The American Frugal Housewife* (Boston, MA, 1832)

Collette, Bruce B., and Grace Klein-MacPhee, *Bigelow and Schroeder's Fishes of the Gulf of Maine* (Washington, DC, 2002)

Collingham, Lizzie, *The Taste of Empire: How Britain's Quest for Food Shaped the Modern World* (New York, 2017)

Cronon, William, *Changes in the Land: Indians, Colonists, and the Ecology of New England* (New York, 1983)

Davidson, Alan, *North Atlantic Seafood* (Berkeley, CA, 2003)

—, *The Oxford Companion to Food* (New York, 2014)

Fagan, Brian, *Fish on Friday: Feasting, Fasting, and the Discovery of the New World* (New York, 2006)

Glasse, Hannah, *The Art of Cookery Made Plain and Easy*
    (London, 1747)
Goldstein, Darra, *Beyond the North Wind: Russia in Recipes and
    Lore* (Berkeley, CA, 2020)
—, *Fire and Ice: Classical Nordic Cooking* (Berkeley, CA, 2015)
Greenberg, Paul, *Four Fish: The Future of the Last Wild Food*
    (New York, 2010)
Grigson, Jane, *Jane Grigson's Fish Book* (London, 1973)
Hilborn, Ray, with Ulrike Hilborn, *Overfishing: What Everyone
    Needs to Know* (Oxford, 2012)
Jensen, Albert C., *The Cod* (New York, 1972)
Kurlansky, Mark, *Cod: A Biography of the Fish that Changed the
    World* (New York, 1997)
—, *Salt: A World History* (New York, 2002)
McGee, Harold, *On Food and Cooking*, 2nd edn (New York
    and London, 2004)
Molokhovets, Elena Ivanovna, *A Gift to Young Housewives*
    (St Petersburg, 1861)
Oliver, Sandra L., *Saltwater Foodways: New Englanders and Their
    Food, at Sea and Ashore, in the Nineteenth Century* (Mystic,
    CT, 1995)
Pye, Michael, *The Edge of the World: A Cultural History of the
    North Sea and the Transformation of Europe* (New York, 2014)
Riely, Elizabeth, *The Chef's Companion* (Hoboken, NJ, 2003)
Rose, George A., ed., *Atlantic Cod: A Bio-Ecology* (Hoboken, NJ,
    2019)
—, *Cod: The Ecological History of the North Atlantic Fisheries*
    (St John's, NL, 2007)
Simmons, Amelia, *American Cookery* (Albany, NY, 1796)
Smith, Andrew F., ed., *The Oxford Companion to American
    Food and Drink* (New York, 2007)
—, *The Oxford Encyclopedia of Food and Drink in America*
    (Oxford, 2004)
Stavely, Keith, and Fitzgerald, Kathleen, *America's Founding
    Food* (Chapel Hill, NC, and London, 2004)
—, *Northern Hospitality: Cooking by the Book in New England*
    (Amherst and Boston, MA, 2011)

Vaughan, Alden T., ed., *New England's Prospect* (Amherst, MA, 1977)

White, Jasper, *50 Chowders: One-Pot Meals – Clam, Corn and Beyond* (New York, 2000)

Wilson, C. Anne, *Food and Drink in Britain: From the Stone Age to Recent Times* (London, 1973)

Websites and Associations

Business Iceland
www.businessiceland.is
https://seafoodfromiceland.com

Darra Goldstein
www.darragoldstein.com

Environmental Defense Fund Seafood Selector
https://seafood.edf.org/cod

ICES Journal of Marine Science
www.academic.oup.com/icesjms

International Council for the Exploration of the Sea
www.ices.dk

Jasper White
www.summershackrestaurant.com

Leite's Culinaria
www.leitesculinaria.com

Marine Conservation Society Good Fish Guide
www.mcsuk.org/goodfishguide

Marine Stewardship Council 'Track a Fishery'
https://fisheries.msc.org/en/fisheries

Monterey Bay Aquarium Seafood Watch
www.seafoodwatch.org

Norwegian Seafood Council
https://en.seafood.no

Portugalia Marketplace for Norwegian and Canadian salt cod
www.portugaliamarketplace.com/collections/
bacalhau-salted-codfish

Seafood from Norway
https://cod.fromnorway.com

Acknowledgements

Elizabeth Gawthrop Riely planned to write this book, but died before she could start it. She helped me get started in journalism in Boston, and was a generous friend and colleague. Beth wrote that 'food is a way of bringing us together', and that is what brought us together. Many thanks to her sons who supported this project and loaned me her culinary library.

It's impossible to write a book like this without tremendous help from others. I am most grateful to Dr George A. Rose, University of British Columbia marine biologist and *Fisheries Research* editor in chief, who read select chapters for scientific accuracy with great care, combined with a sense of humour and curiosity. I am also indebted to Dr Reidar Bertelsen, historical archaeologist, University of Tromsø, who shared his research on Norway's fisher-farmer economy; and Dr Trevor Branch, associate professor at the University of Washington School of Aquatic and Fishery Sciences, who first recommended Dr Rose and additional resources.

I have received much generosity of spirit from culinary colleagues: Dr Jessica B. Harris shared her ackee and saltfish recipe; Janet P. Boileau sent me her dissertation – a culinary history of the Portuguese Eurasians; Colleen Taylor Sen provided information about Goan salt cod cuisine; Darra Goldstein, professor of Russian, emerita at Williams College, was invaluable in her advice regarding Russian cuisine; Sandy Oliver gave an enlightening explanation of cod heads as dining-table centrepieces that supplemented her essential New England seafood book; David Leite generously elaborated on his Portuguese salt cod knowledge and shared recipes and photographs; and Jasper White for his scrumptious chowder recipe. And always, Andy Smith, who first invited me to write about lobster and now cod, offered dependable support throughout the writing of this book.

And a huge shout out to the incomparable librarians at the Concord Free Public Library, the Boston Public Library and the Schlesinger Library.

Thanks to Björgvin Þór Björgvinsson, Business Iceland, and Anette Grøttland Zimowski and Kari-Anne Johansen, Norwegian Seafood Council, who patiently answered questions and furnished excellent photos and recipes. Also, I'm grateful to Jennifer Walsh at the Newfoundland and Labrador Department of Fisheries, Forestry and Agriculture for recipes. Many thanks to Alisha Lumea at Wulf's Fish for great photos. Finally, many people from the Norwegian museums helped, but Curator Bjørn Djupevåg from the Norwegian Fisheries Museum provided the incredible historical Norwegian photos.

Others have been invaluable in so many ways – to my translators Grace Butler, Nora Cyra, Nune Hakobyan and Laurie Van Loon. Also, Lisa Townsend, Suzanne Lowe, Anne Fortier, Katharine Esty, Squamies, Fran Grigsby, Jane Fisher, Ann Willard, C. C. King, Claire Muhm, Sargis Karapetyan, Narayan Helen Liebenson, Carin Roberge, Mary Jo Alexander, George Klavens, Karen Carlson, Jeff Robichaud, Titilayo Alabi and, last but not least, my Concord writers' group.

I have been continuously buoyed by the love, steadfast support and brillance of my husband Jeff Greene, and my sixteen-year-old bichon frisé and daily companion Reny.

Photo Acknowledgements

The author and publishers wish to express their thanks to the below sources of illustrative material and/or permission to reproduce it. Some locations of artworks are also given below, in the interest of brevity:

Albertina Museum, Vienna: p. 23; Bonnefantenmuseum, Maastricht (on loan from Rijksdienst voor het Cultureel Erfgoed, Amersfoort): p. 16; photo Peter Bösken/Pixabay: p. 30; Boston Public Library: p. 43; courtesy Business Iceland: pp. 23, 35, 36, 46 (photo Antonio Saba), 76, 92, 98 (photo Pepe Brix), 99, 106 (photo Pepe Brix), 107, 113; photo Daderot: p. 42; courtesy Gulf of Maine Research Institute, Portland, ME: p. 18; James Ford Bell Library, University of Minnesota, Minneapolis: p. 63; courtesy David Leite and Leite's Culinaria, https://leitesculinaria.com: pp. 70, 71; Library Company of Philadelphia, PA: p. 59; Library of Congress, Prints and Photographs Division, Washington, DC: p. 58; courtesy Alisha Lumea/Wulf's Fish: pp. 80, 87 (*bottom*); courtesy Marine Stewardship Council (MSC): p. 121; NASA/Goddard Space Flight Center (GSFC)/Langley Research Center (LARC)/JPL, MISR Team: p. 22; Nasjonalbiblioteket, Oslo: pp. 32, 108; courtesy National Museum of Iceland, Reykjavík: p. 11; The New York Public Library: p. 14; NOAA Photo Library (crew and officers of NOAA Ship *Miller Freeman*): p. 90; Norsk Folkemuseum, Oslo: pp. 10, 15, 37, 93; Norsk Teknisk Museum, Oslo: p. 111; © Norwegian Seafood Council: pp. 31 (*bottom*; photo Johan Wildhagen), 47, 82 (photo James Eric

Hensley/Studio Dreyer-Hensley), 83 (photo Gudrun Hoffmann and Ulla Westbø (H2W)), 87 (*top*; photo Fabian Bjørnstjerna); PhotoVisions/Shutterstock.com: p. 6; private collection: pp. 39, 57, 61; South Street Seaport Museum, New York: p. 120; from Lindsay G. Thompson, *History of the Fisheries of New South Wales* (Sydney, 1893), photo State Library of Pennsylvania, Harrisburg: p. 48; photo Elisabeth Townsend: p. 101.

but not in any way that suggests the licensor endorses you or your use; share alike – If you remix, transform, or build upon the material, you must distribute your contributions under the same license as the original.

Index

italic numbers refer to illustrations; **bold** to recipes